APPEAL TO THE HEART

ESPECIALLY FOR GIRLS™ presents

APPEAL TO THE HEART

J. Marlin

PACER BOOKS

a member of The Putnam Publishing Group
New York

This book is a presentation of Especially for Girls™, Weekly
Reader Books. Weekly Reader Books offers book clubs for
children from preschool through high school. For
further information write to: **Weekly Reader Books,**
4343 Equity Drive, Columbus, Ohio 43228.

Especially for Girls™ is a trademark
of Weekly Reader Books.

Edited for Weekly Reader Books and published by
arrangement with Pacer Books.

Published by Pacer Books,
a member of The Putnam Publishing Group
51 Madison Avenue
New York, New York 10010

Library of Congress Cataloging-in-Publication Data
Marlin, J.
    Appeal to the heart.
    Summary: Serving as Chief Justice in a mock court
for her high school law course, Sandrine finds her
decision affected by her emotional involvement with
both student lawyers.
[1. Courts—Fiction. 2. High schools—Fiction.
3. Schools—Fiction] I. Title.
PZ7.M3446Ap 1986 [Fic] 85-12386
ISBN 0-448-47769-6

For George and Loretta

APPEAL TO THE HEART

1.

I couldn't help laughing out loud.

This was by far the funniest comic strip Reed Hobart had ever drawn.

Jan saw me giggling, leaned on the shiny brown wall beside me, and peeked at my copy of *The Green Park Planet*, our school newspaper. Soon Jan was laughing louder than I. We'd been friends for two years, and once in a while our laughter got out of hand. *She* usually started it. Most of the time I did my best to keep from getting dragged in. Jan was the fun-loving one, not me.

Today we were laughing in front of Mr. Bain's classroom. He teaches Social Studies and we were taking a senior elective called Law and Democracy. I was determined *not* to take my giggles into class.

Although Jan did not especially mind people staring at her, I hated being the center of attention.

"Enjoying yourselves?"

I lowered the paper. Reed Hobart stood in front

of me, six feet tall, eyebrows raised over clear hazel eyes, angular features forming a crooked grin. My laughter ended abruptly, in a gulp.

"Great strip," Jan gasped. "The best."

Reed's long face tilted toward me as his soft voice deepened an octave. "And what does my worst critic say?"

"It's all right for what it is."

Jan sighed impatiently. I knew I could count on another lecture demanding I "stop playing infantile games." She meant trading insults with Reed. Jan had other plans for us.

"See you inside." She winked significantly.

"That's all?" Reed asked, challenging me. "Just all right?"

"It'll do." I half-smiled. "It's pretty funny." His jaw dropped in mock surprise. His knee touched the floor as he made a low bow, arms outstretched like balancing poles.

"Well, thank *you*, Queen Sandrine."

Pete "The Bone" Sweeney and some of his low-life friends walked past us on their way into the room. Pete glanced at Reed and snickered to his pals.

"Get up," I whispered, infuriated by even a little unwanted attention.

Reed stood, pointing a huge, obnoxious finger. "The trouble with you is, you don't have a decent sense of humor."

Just then, Ted Steele swaggered toward us between two empty-eyed cheerleaders, one of them seemingly hypnotized by his curly blue-black hair and heart-attack handsome smile.

"What's happening, Speedo?" Ted grinned.

Lacrosse players called Reed "Speedo" because he's so slow. He's great at blocking shots but not much at running, which is why he went out for goal.

I knew the bell must have already rung, because Ted Steele never got to Law and Democracy class on time. Most often he made his big entrance a minute after the bell.

Seeing Ted ahead of me inspired mild panic at the idea of all those eyes following me to my seat. Still, I wasn't about to let "Speedo" off with that attack on my sense of humor. I started to tell him he'd need more than pathetic jokes to pull him through what would certainly be a submediocre life. But before I got very far, Mr. Bain's silver crew cut and horn-rimmed glasses emerged from the doorway. *He* has a sense of humor you have to watch out for.

Mr. Bain smiled innocently and said in his slow Georgia drawl, "Could I possibly impose on you all to join our little group for the next forty minutes?"

"We were arguing capital punishment," Reed mumbled, heading into the room.

"No doubt," Mr. Bain sighed. "Sandrine? Will you come aboard as well?"

I hadn't moved yet because I was too embarrassed. More specifically, I felt a blush invade my cheeks. Mr. Bain lifted one thick silver eyebrow and nodded toward the room. I walked to my seat with the grace of a tall, yellow-haired marionette being jerked around. The blush burned my forehead as I sat.

Mr. Bain held up his own copy of *The Green Park Planet*. It was folded to show the editorial page, and Reed's comic strip, "Fools 'n' Tools." All the characters in Fools 'n' Tools were turtles. A turtle's the symbol of Green Park High, same as the nearby University where I had already applied for the following September. Reed's turtles sported familiar faces: teachers, students, administrators. That week's star turtle was more outrageous than most. In fact, I was slightly amazed that it hadn't been censored. Here was a bug-eyed creature wearing Dean Benoit's shaggy moustache. The strip showed him sneaking all over school, checking people's program cards. The last box pictured him getting booted out of the girls' locker room on the end of Miss Hufty's oversized sneaker.

Mr. Bain tapped a finger to his lips, and the class began to quiet down. "I take it some of the ladies and gentlemen contend that our honored administration erred in suspending so many friends and colleagues?"

Those who understood, nodded. The rest took their cue from us. If he catches you not understanding him, watch out for that sense of humor.

About five months earlier, late in October, a senior who worked for the guidance office and desperately wanted to be a school legend went to the

University printing shop and had a rubber stamp made. It said, "Program Change Approved" and looked exactly like the real thing. Then he started stamping program cards for friends who were dissatisfied.

Suddenly, people began substituting lunch for classes and going home early. Others dropped subjects like Math for Ethnic Cooking or Pottery-Making.

By the time the school computer electronically sniffed something funny, all kinds of people had stopped by the office to make use of the new service. Then, just last week, after checking out every program change since the fall, the administration gave two-day suspensions to fifty-three kids including Jan's boyfriend, Bronto.

Green Park High still quivered with the shock.

What was Mr. Bain going to say? And why was he waving a comic strip around? I anticipated words of wisdom on freedom of the press.

He began, "Our friend Mr. Hobart has a gift for making us laugh, and for driving a sharp point home as he does. But how will lampooning Dean Benoit help anyone understand the issues in this case?"

He looked around. Jan turned a blank face to me. In classes where I was especially good, like this one or English Lit or Theories of the Mind, I often passed Jan little notes with questions on them, combining my knowledge with her talent for public speaking. Not today. I saw Reed studying Mr. Bain. Handsome Ted Steele was too busy delighting a lively redhead to notice much of anything.

"No thoughts?" Mr. Bain taunted. A couple of hands tested the air, then dropped. Jan stuck hers straight up. She's got more guts than the Baltimore fish market.

"It shows we think the administration was wrong, even if we can't do anything about it."

An approving murmur followed. Mr. Bain juggled his eyebrows happily, now that he'd begun to win our interest.

He said, "Don't bet that you can't do anything," and hooked both skinny thumbs into the pockets of his butterscotch corduroy vest. "Anything else? Sandrine?"

"No, really," I pleaded, struggling to keep my voice audible. I knew why he'd called on me. At the top of my last report he'd written, "You have an original, interesting mind. Try sharing it through class participation."

I did try. I just didn't succeed.

Mr. Bain continued, "We are going to explore the matter of the fifty-three suspensions in this class. Dean Benoit has agreed to join us as a witness, if called."

Suddenly, *everyone* listened closely. This sounded like a definite improvement over the Attica Prison Riots we were supposed to study next week. Even Ted Steele and the redhead paid attention.

Mr. Bain explained, "We are going to hold a Court of Appeals. We will have a legal team of three lawyers to challenge the administration's action. Another three-lawyer team will defend the administration. A five-judge panel will write an opinion. Those who do not become lawyers or judges will each write a two-page opinion based on the evidence presented. These will be *graded*. We will have witnesses and rules. The entire exercise will take two weeks. Preparations will start on Monday. Court will convene a week from Monday, and will be held in the Small Auditorium. Is that clear?"

Not a peep.

"Good," Mr. Bain said, handing scrap paper to the first person in each row. "If you wish to participate, print your name and the role you'd like to play. Oh, yes, there will be a chief attorney to lead each legal team and a chief justice to lead the court. Remember, print clearly."

I looked around. Jan, Reed and about half the class including Ted Steele scribbled intently. Of course, I did not even consider it. That's all I'd need, sitting there in the Small Auditorium, in front of everyone, blushing like a stoplight!

"Sorry I made you late," Reed rumbled. I was a few feet outside Mr. Bain's room when he caught up with me, looking more amused than sorry.

"That's okay." I tried for bored.

"Have a nice weekend." He hesitated, waved, and walked away.

"You, too," I replied, cool as lemon ice.

Ordinarily, last period Friday was Vocabulary Club for us both, except when Reed had a game.

Mrs. Greenwhit sicked out that day though, so the club meeting was cancelled. Being a senior honor student, I could've gone home, but I didn't feel very much like it.

Ted Steele dashed past Reed shouting, "Race you to the lockers." I saw Reed slump as Ted ducked through the far stairwell door.

Jan must've been watching me watch Reed.

"I'm gonna hang out at practice," she said. "Want to come?"

"Why not?"

Here in Maryland, lacrosse is considered more essential to life than oxygen, although in most other places nobody's heard of it.

Each lacrosse team has ten players who carry plastic sticks three- to six-feet-long with small triangle-shaped nets on the ends. They run up and down a football-sized field wearing helmets and big gloves and hitting each other with the sticks. They also use the sticks to carry a baseball-sized solid rubber ball, pass it back and forth, and try to shoot it into the other team's goal, which is six feet square and guarded by a heavily padded goalie.

Jan's boyfriend Bronto was captain and our top defenseman, Ted Steele led the attack, and Reed tended the goal.

"What's on your mind?" Jan asked as we watched thirty bare-legged marvels snort and groan through push-ups. A bright blue sky vibrated over the green playing field. Whiffs of salty bay water came and went. I didn't have to tell Jan I wanted to talk. And, being the kind of best friend anyone would hope for, she knew I'd need help.

"Anything new with your stepmom-to-be?" she asked.

I shook my head.

"You depressed?"

I shook my head again. Since my doomed romance of last summer, I'd spent some time in a depression Jan called "the black hole of woe." If you've ever felt so bad you were afraid to go to sleep because you couldn't stand waking up, you know what I mean. Those interludes used to last two days, sometimes three. But I hadn't had any since Christmas.

"You want to talk about Reed?" Jan asked.

"Do you?" I imitated her low, sympathetic voice. That didn't bother Jan. She rolled her eyes and said, "He likes you, that's absolutely obvious. And you like him too, even if you won't admit it."

"I don't know," I said.

"C'mon, Sandrine. Everyone *knows* about him. Why do you think he joined that bizarre Vocabulary Club?"

"How should I know?"

"Because *you're* in it. Why else? You *know* all this. We've been through it nine dozen times."

"If he likes me so much, why doesn't he fall down at my feet or something?"

Reed and I had hardly known each other until

the end of last August when my boyfriend, Ron, introduced us at the lake. They'd worked on *The Green Park Planet* together.

Reed had a reputation for saying funny, satirical things, but he hardly said any to me. Most of the time he seemed nervous, searching for words. I suspected he might be interested, but Ron was about to move away and that was all I could think about.

After Ron left and I started getting depressed, Reed and I still said hello. I looked forward to seeing him in school. We never talked much, but it always relaxed me a little. I told Jan it was like having a brother my own age. She has two and said it's entirely different.

Things went on that way through most of the fall. Reed would spot me in the hall, come over and say, "How are you doing today?" I'd tell him I felt okay, whether I did or not. He'd ask if I'd heard from Ron, and I'd say I had. We'd talk about Ron, or something else. Then he'd nod and shrug, or smile, and walk away.

Toward the end of October, he joined Vocabulary Club. Once, in early November, he mumbled ten words about going to the movies and I looked the other way. I was deep in a "black hole of woe" at the time. I still remember him making a joke about my excusing his temporary insanity. At about that time, he began acting weird, speaking sarcastically, pulling silly stunts like the one outside Mr. Bain's room.

It was April now, and he had never asked me out

again. I pretty much assumed he never would.

Jan was saying how you couldn't expect every guy in the world to be as mature as Bronto (Bertram) Gould. She cast an adoring eye at the two-hundred-thirty-pound love of her life as he led his men in lung-pumping jumping jacks.

"Guess not," I agreed.

"Reed needs encouragement, ever hear of it?" Jan wrinkled her forehead. "He's a creative person, after all. Who knows what goes through a creative person's mind?"

"Or a goalie's," I agreed.

Twenty yards away, Ted Steele twisted around Bronto and fired the ball at the goalie's head. Reed flicked his stick up to catch it, then waited for the next attacker to rush at him and shoot.

If that goalie/cartoonist needed encouragement, I knew he could have a long wait. Encouraging wasn't exactly my major strength. Insulting came more naturally. Besides, I asked myself half-heartedly, who said I was *pining* for him anyway?

Only Jan. And she could be wrong.

2.

Bob and Brenda, my twin siblings, were seven.

Like me, they have our mother's gray-green eyes, blond hair and small nose. Brenda is thoroughly beautiful. Bob is perfectly pleasant-looking. That's how I think of myself.

When I got home that afternoon, they sat on the curb in front of our white stucco house, wearing winter coats and furious faces.

"We can't use the computer," Bob growled before I had a chance to ask what was wrong.

"Yeah," Brenda chimed in several notes higher, "Mrs. Binder won't let us."

I could easily imagine what had happened. Bob had wanted to play Universal Destruction. Brenda had insisted on High-Power Math. Neither would give in. They started screaming, their voices getting louder. Mrs. Binder's patience stretched and snapped, at which point she kicked them out, saying, "Hooligans don't play computer games. Not in this house they don't."

"Come on inside." I took a small, cold hand in each of mine.

Mrs. Binder is shaped like a beach ball. She's short, but must weigh two hundred pounds. It hasn't affected her health, though, or slowed her down at all. The woman is always in motion, singing "Stardust," talking to herself, patting her thick, white hair to keep it neat, smoothing her yellow smock. When we walked in, she was cutting up vegetables, mixing dressing, basting the roast and getting her biscuit batter together.

I'd told the twins what to do.

"We're sorry we were hooligans," Bob muttered, looking everywhere but at her. "We're sorry we gave you a headache."

"Really and truly," Brenda chirped. "If we're ever hooligans again, you can stick us in the oven."

I hadn't told her to put it exactly like that. Mrs. Binder stopped shredding purple cabbage. She bent forward, shaking her head. They were home free. She caught one kid in each arm, squeezed and pointed a stubby finger up at me. "Can you keep these hooligans quiet?"

"Yes, ma'am." Then, looking at the food, I asked, "Maddie coming for dinner?"

Mrs. Binder straightened up, fists on hips. "Yes. And I hope you will be nice to her."

"I'm always nice to her," I protested.

"You know plain enough what I mean."

I did, too. Mrs. Binder hoped I would show Maddie some affection. As Mrs. B. often said, "It's long past time you welcomed her into this family."

Easier said than done. Since I'd overcome my jealousy in November, I had nothing against my stepmom-to-be. In fact, I'd begun to like her. But affection? Well, I often planned a little hello kiss. I'd imagine her coming through the door. I'd see myself reaching out. Thinking about it was simple enough. But doing it?

I couldn't.

Since my father and Maddie started dating two years ago, she'd always used the most powerful psychological weapon known to the human race. Bringing presents. Not that the kids liked her only for that. They loved her, period. Still, presents make the feet beat faster down the stairs, which they did at six thirty as the car pulled into the driveway.

I was on the living room couch reading up on flatworms for bio, the field in which I intend to major at college. I tried to picture giving Maddie a casual hug, like on a talk show.

My father, Sam J. Lang, is Vice President for Marketing at Shore Foods Inc., a division of North American Products, and the makers of world-famous Chesapeake Brand frozen crabcakes. He is responsible for all their advertising, and the way their boxes look, and how they test out new brainstorms (such as the extremely popular Cheddar Delight crabcake) to see which ones America wants to eat most.

Maddie is in charge of Human Resources Development for the same company, and also a V.P. She decides who gets hired for executive and sales positions. Also, she dreams up executive and sales training courses on how to "think crabcakes," how to boss people around but still have them like you, and how to relax under pressure so you don't get a heart attack.

They make a nice-looking couple. My father, Sam J., is tall, with salt-and-pepper hair, blue eyes and a long, thin nose. Maddie is average height with dark curly hair, a wide mouth and round, golden eyes.

The twins jumped all over them and Maddie gave Bob a box, saying, "This is for you both. Share nicely or I may decide to keep it for myself." Maddie would have taken it back if they started fighting over it.

Maddie never brought anything for me because, back when I was still jealous and filled with resentment, I refused a present and told her I didn't want any. She knew my feelings had changed somewhat since then, but I guess she wasn't taking chances and stayed with the no-gift policy.

Instead she threw me a wave and a smile, which I returned.

My father came over to kiss my head.

"Pot roast for dinner," I reported.

"But it won't be ready for half an hour," Mrs.

Binder shouted from the kitchen, "so you'd better think of something to talk about until then."

Bob and Brenda tore their gift from its wrapper—a computer game called Galloping Gaucho. They galloped upstairs to try it.

I put away my bio book and prepared to chat. Since I couldn't think of anything else, I described the Court of Appeals.

"Sounds great," my father said. "Too bad you won't participate. Terrible waste of a brilliant young mind."

Maddie got him off that by asking about the case, which I summarized.

"Do you have an opinion?" she asked.

"Well," I said, "I don't know if it's so hot to put suspensions in everybody's record for a thing like that, but it's hard to know what I'd do if I were the administration."

"Two sides to everything, right?" Sam J. smiled.

I nodded.

After dinner we all watched TV together. Maddie tried to discuss wedding plans with me, but I just could not show interest. That was a little like hugging her. I wanted to, and I knew I should. But wanting and doing are two different things.

"Have you any plans for the weekend?" she asked before my father drove her home.

"Not yet," I answered.

Maddie seemed to feel responsible for keeping me occupied. Not so much at night, but on weekend afternoons. Since I stopped hating her, they tried to include me with the twins. I didn't mind tagging along to zoos, museums, wherever. I never had a really great time, but I did feel sort of protected.

Lately though, I liked spending more and more time alone. So when my father suggested I join them for a trip to the good old Smithsonian in Washington, D.C., I told him I expected other things to happen. Not that I did. Jan was booked solid with Bronto all weekend and nobody else had invited me anywhere. I enjoyed myself anyway. I studied, did some early work in the garden, and played computer games—Universal Destruction, High-Power Math, and mostly Galloping Gaucho.

At school on Monday, I was surprised to find many people talking about "the Court." Who would be the lawyers? Who would be the judges? From what I soon gathered, *no* one had volunteered to defend the administration. Most people wanted to be judges. Why? They figured all they'd have to do would be to sit back and listen.

Of course, *nobody* wanted to get stuck writing two-page opinions, which nonparticipators had to do. Therefore, the people who didn't sign up tended to be shy (like me) or too insecure to see themselves as judges or lawyers.

I looked forward to the spectacle. Something told me our two prize bigmouths, Reed "Creative" Hobart and Ted "Hollywood-Model" Steele, would wind up team leaders. Otherwise, they'd battle to take over any team they ended up on.

I knew Jan wanted to be a judge and I hoped Mr. Bain would have the sense to make her one.

Without Reed Hobart pestering me in the hall, I got to my seat nice and early. I had to stand because as people entered, they hung around the front, blocking my view of the chalkboard. Mr. Bain wrote: "Legal Team Advancing the Appeal" on the blackboard. Then he wrote the names of Richie Green and superbrain Sheila Dufay. Above their names he wrote: "Chief Attorney, Mr. R. Hobart."

Reed walked in at that moment, made a supposedly comical face and ambled back to his seat. He flung a gloat at me, but I kept my eyes on the chalkboard.

The front of the room had become jammed and Mr. Bain stopped writing. "I am duly impressed with your loitering skills," he said. "Now, be so good as to sit."

Everyone walked backward, as though the names on the board might change if not watched closely. Ted arrived on time, quietly, flirting with no one.

Mr. Bain wrote: "Legal Team Defending the Administration Against the Appeal." A few people booed.

"Now that you've aired your loftiest thoughts," Mr. Bain drawled, "please refrain from further infantilisms."

He stared until the offenders nodded agreement. Subdued snickers greeted the two defense lawyers' names, and the only vulgar noise occurred when Mr. Bain finished writing, "Chief Attorney, Mr. T. Steele."

Thirty disgusted faces turned Ted's way. He grinned like the worm who'd discovered dirt. I assumed he'd volunteered for the proadministration side so he could be Chief Attorney without competition.

"How come both of the chiefs are guys?" asked Sheila Dufay.

"Wait," smiled Mr. Bain, turning to write again.

My heart skipped a beat. I considered Jan a cinch for Chief Justice. Her name hadn't turned up yet, and Bain *had* to make the one remaining chief a girl. What's more, she was smart, mature, outspoken...everything you could want in a Chief Justice. She winked at me. I was so happy for her!

Once again, he started at the bottom of the list. He wrote Jan's name third out of five, eliminating her for Chief Justice. I was horrified. Nobody else had *nearly* her brains or personality. She looked at me with a cheerful "win some, lose some" smile, proving what a good-natured, feet-on-the-ground person she is. I was so busy fuming with outrage that I failed to notice Mr. Bain writing the fourth lawyer's name.

Not until he'd finished lettering "Chief Justice" did I return my eyes to the board. Even before he actually wrote my name, I knew. And a second later, there it was: "Ms. S. Lang."

I struggled to force air past the very large boulder plugging my throat. Every vein and capillary between scalp and shoulders filled with boiling lava. I heard everyone whispering, "blushshshinnng" all around me.

I forced myself to look in Jan's direction, hoping to find comfort in the sight of a loyal, friendly face. I did *not* expect to see her wavy brown hair and tanned arms resting on her desk top as her shoulders quivered with laughter!

After devoting a few painful moments to breathing, I raised burning eyes to see Mr. Bain smile calmly and ask the class to please stop staring at me. Next, my anguished glance fell on Reed. His jaw hung open, unhinged by amazement. *Catching flies for lunch?* I thought, despite my distress. Ted Steele seemed to be waving. I blinked him into focus.

"Congratulations," he whispered.

Jan finally managed to stop giggling and timidly peeked over. I decided to ignore her for the rest of the day.

I also decided to put a quick stop to this absolute injustice. The moment the class ended, I'd certainly set Mr. Bain straight.

"Apparently you do not know it," I imagined myself telling him in a superpolite tone, "but I did not, in reality, write my name on any of your scrap paper. No, Mr. Bain, I did not volunteer for anything, much less Chief Justice. I would recommend Janet

Robbins for the job, but her brain has recently decomposed. Still, you may want to ask her tomorrow—if she recovers."

"I'm sorry. I'm really sorry," Jan whispered, biting her lower lip as she stood by my desk the moment Mr. Bain excused the class.

I junked my polite tone and whispered, "I've never been so embarrassed in my life. How could you laugh? How could you *possibly* laugh when I practically had three strokes from embarrassment? Didn't you see how I was blushing?"

"I couldn't help it," Jan squeaked. She was about to do it again.

"Go perch," I told her, more disgusted than ever by her struggle to stifle a fresh flood of giggles. Moments later, I joined the three students already leaning over Mr. Bain's desk.

One was Richie Green, a shy, stoop-shouldered guy who wears thick glasses and used to stutter badly. When I got there, Mr. Bain had told the others to give Richie a chance.

"I want you to know it's okay if you don't really want me to be on the lawyer team," Green said slowly, but without any stammer.

"Not at all." Mr. Bain looked and sounded surprised, as though he couldn't imagine why such a thing would occur to Richie Green.

"If you think I might get nervous and have a problem speaking or something like that," Richie said.

"Oh, I see." Mr. Bain looked at me for some reason, then at Green. "Richie, you and Sheila will decide what you want your role on the team to be. I picked you because you have the intellectual equipment to make a superior contribution. Is that clear?"

You don't often get to see Richie Green smile, but I did then, and it was quite nice.

The other two were not moved. Both were members of Ted Steele's defense team. And both wanted out. It seems they'd written "lawyer" on their scrapsheets, but neglected to say which kind of lawyer they preferred to be. Since no one except Ted Steele actually volunteered to stand up for Dean Benoit, these two were the best Mr. Bain could do.

"It's not fair," complained chubby Arnold Playfield, who'd have made the Honor Society if eating skills counted.

"I don't even think you can do that," added Lisa Hooper, a small energetic girl who played girls' varsity volleyball and reported on games for *The Green Park Planet*, giving herself star billing.

Mr. Bain eyed them coolly. "Well," he purred, "this is certainly a free country. And the class *is* Law and Democracy. So I guess we *had* better be fair and democratic about it, hmmmnnn?"

They nodded.

As I rehearsed my statement, Mr. Bain bribed my two classmates by pointing out that this assignment could be just the thing to sparkle up their unfortunate grades. Young Playfield might even look forward to passing the course.

Arnold had begun a string of Thank-you-sir's when

I heard someone calling me. Ted Steele beckoned from the hall.

Needless to say, he'd never so much as noticed my existence before today, much less beckoned. I ignored him. Settling matters with Mr. Bain was all I cared about.

Lisa was haggling for a guaranteed B+ when a firm yet gentle hand grasped my upper arm.

Ted whispered huskily, "I need to talk to you … *now.*"

I admit that sent a shiver down my spine.

3.

Ted Steele is the sort of person who gets whatever he wants from life. The main reason is that it's all he thinks about. The other reasons are that he is very smart and too gorgeous to be true.

I let him guide me into the hall, telling myself I'd catch Mr. Bain before he left the room.

Ted and I are both five-nine, so I found myself looking directly into his dark blue eyes.

"Yes?" I asked, aware that I did not sound as impatient as I intended.

"I just want you to know how much I look forward to working with you."

"Thank you," I said. "So do I."

"Working with me, you mean?"

"Right." I felt a giggle begin, and strangled it.

"I know you'll do a great job." Ted never blinked or took his eyes from mine.

I replied, "Dean Benoit needs all the help he can get."

"Can't give in to the rabble, can we?"

"The who?" I had trouble concentrating. For one thing, my heart was hammering like the motor of Bronto's ancient Buick. For another, I was blushing, again.

Ted seemed to overlook my glow. "The rabble," he clarified, "the mob, the common folk."

"Oh, them," I said.

"Can't let savage emotions tear down civilization," he pointed out.

"No," I agreed.

Then Ted explained that when it came to choosing between law and democracy, he liked law better. After a minute or so of that, still not letting go of my eyes, he flashed his amazingly white teeth and said, "Well, plenty of time to talk about such things in the future. Hey, Sandy, what are you doing after school today?"

Sandy? No one had ever called me that. It was a new name.

"Huh?" My heart thudded into third gear.

"After school. How about you be my guest at practice today? And after, we can go to Lou's for a burger and discuss these fascinating topics to our heart's content."

I gazed at him.

"How about it?" he asked.

"Um, no. Thanks. I don't think so."

I was *trying* to say that I had no intention of appearing as Chief Justice, Assistant Justice or any other kind of Justice. Ted, of course, assumed I was turning him down. Instead of getting upset or discouraged, he smiled more beautifully than ever and said, "Better things to do with your time? Hey, I'm not surprised. Maybe later. See you tomorrow, Sandy."

It didn't take me too long to recover. Once my heart slowed down to seminormal, I tried to reenter Mr. Bain's room. It was locked. I hated to think that Ted Steele's performance had so distracted me that I missed Mr. Bain's departure. But I didn't have much choice.

In a flash I realized how wrong I had been, acting so mean to my best friend, Jan. I probably *did* look silly gasping for air when Mr. Bain wrote my name on the board. Certainly Jan had meant no harm.

The main thing at *that* point was, I needed to talk to her fast. I had the feeling that things were going just slightly out of control. Where was she?

I asked myself that for the twentieth time outside the door leading to the locker rooms (boys to the right, girls to the left), when Reed jumped down the last five steps of the staircase from the front hall.

"Well, well, well," he repeated as though it was something the world wanted to hear several times. I didn't bother to answer.

He smiled. "Looks like we'll have to call a truce."

"A truce?" I replied. "I didn't know anyone fired a shot."

He clutched his stomach and staggered, pretending my latest blast had penetrated his guts.

"Have you seen Jan?" I asked, as long as he was there.

"Nope. But listen, if you want to be perfectly fair as Chief Justice, we should try to cut down on these hostile conversations we've been having lately."

"Oh, really?"

"Yeah. Absolutely."

I took a long, deep breath. Then I told him, "It may interest you to know that first, I am not going to *be* on the stupid court. Some nitwit forged my name on one of those scrap sheets, and as soon as I tell Mr. Bain, this little mistake will be history."

"And second?"

"Second what?" I asked impatiently.

"You said, 'First I am not going to be on the stupid court.' What's second?"

He really can drive a sane person crazy.

"Second," I said wearily, "even if I *did* happen to be on some bizarre court like this, I'm *sure* I could be completely fair no matter *how* hostile I feel toward the lawyers, *or* how *annoying* they turned out to be."

"That's no way to talk about poor Teddy Steele."

Something came over me when he said that. My voice became positively intense. "Ted Steele is not annoying. Just exactly the opposite. I think Ted is very, very nice."

"Really?" he said.

"Yes, really."

"Oh, well, uh...sorry I bothered you." Reed turned

his head and walked stiffly through the door to the lockers. I knew I could have handled it better. Even then I understood there was more to Reed's foolishness than met the eye. If I'd been warmer, or more experienced, maybe I could have helped him along. That was Jan's big theory. But I wasn't, so I couldn't. Instead, I let anger dull any hint of regret.

After all, I told myself yet another time, Reed was a major personality in school, what with his cartoons, and all-league goaltending, and well-known opinions on everything from politics to rock 'n' roll. Although he didn't attract the beauty queens who went after Ted, he wasn't exactly starved for female companions. When I saw him with girls, he seemed normal enough. Not that that made me jealous. But why did he have to reserve his goofball act for me?

The more I thought about it, the angrier I got. Reed and I had been getting to know each other, bit by bit, for months—and he hadn't gotten *anywhere*. But in five minutes flat, Ted Steele had invited me to watch practice and have a burger after. What's more, he'd affected my heartbeat and started me hoping that he would ask again. I knew all about his reputation for breaking hearts and being in love exclusively with himself. But that was not the point. At least he could make something happen.

The type of soup on that evening's dinner table made little difference to me. My appetite was weakened by worry. I did not look forward to telling Mr.

Bain I quit, *or* waiting around to see if Ted Steele would give me another try. On top of which, my anger at Reed was giving way to guilt. I wondered if I'd really hurt his feelings, and if I had, how much?

"You feel okay?" my father asked as I picked at my romaine and artichoke salad. Before I could answer, the phone rang. He paused, expecting a call from Maddie. Mrs. Binder picked it up in the kitchen.

"For you, Sandrine. Should I tell this fellow to call back after dinner?"

My father took one look at my face and said, "No, Mrs. Binder, she'll take it now." Then he whispered, "Use the living room phone. More privacy."

En route to the phone I prayed, "Let it be Mr. Bain apologizing for his mistake. Let it be that some numbskull called Mr. Bain at home and confessed to forging my name..."

"You've been on my mind all day." Ted's voice sounded even huskier on the phone than it did in person.

"Hum?" My heart started up again.

He said, "I've been wondering where we're going Friday night. If it wasn't for my aunt Norma's anniversary party, I'd be thinking about Saturday night, too."

"You would?"

"You wanna see Sulfuric Acid? They're playing at Dark in the Park this weekend."

"I don't know." I tried to keep my voice steady. "I don't have an I.D."

"Then how about the Brutal Monkeys concert flick?"

"Well…"

"Great. It's a date. And listen, I just got a call from old Bain-brain."

Was it possible? Had Mr. Bain told Ted to tell me I *didn't* have to be on the court after all? That it was only an amusing error? Why wouldn't Mr. Bain call me himself? Too embarrassed? Too cheap? Too tired?

"Sandrine?" Ted said, "You still there?"

"More or less. Ted, I really have to tell you…"

"I know how you feel, babe. We can talk about it tomorrow. That's what I have to pass along. The meeting's going to be in Bain's office on the second floor, not in the classroom."

The angel of disappointment crash-landed on my shoulder. "Meeting?" I asked.

"You, me and Speedo. The meeting Bain talked about in class."

"I don't remember."

Ted spoke in a confidential tone that made me feel less foolish. "Oh. Well, I guess you were too excited. The three of us are supposed to talk about ground rules. For the Court of Appeals. Just a quick meeting in his office. Second floor. Got that?"

"I guess so."

"Hey, that's great. Sweet dreams, Sweetdream."

"Good night," I said.

"Hurry up or your crab bisque will get cold," my

father warbled from the dining room table.

I forced myself to eat a couple of chicken breasts and a speck of broccoli with cheese sauce. Halfway through my second helping, I remembered what had happened to Jan. Her mother picked her up early from school to go buy contact lenses and then join her Pop downtown for dinner. She'd told me in the morning, but I'd forgotten.

"What's wrong now?" Sam J. asked as I winced at my own absent-mindedness.

My father's a wonderful man. After my mother died five years ago, he held the family together, taking care of me and the twins and himself just about single-handedly. Best of all, he interviewed around five hundred people before he picked Mrs. Binder. I know it got to be very hard work, but he wouldn't stop looking until he found *exactly* the right person. He also worked hard learning about how girls dress and what they like to do and all. He quit being Sales Manager at Shore Foods so he wouldn't have to travel any more. In fact, he's done everything for us that I could imagine.

But I can't claim he has much talent for listening to personal problems and giving advice. He's more into saying things like, "It'll all work out," or "Wish I could help you more," or "You've got the right idea, Sandrine. Follow your instincts."

And once he says that, you get the feeling *he* thinks he's solved the problem. Don't misunderstand. I never resented that about him. But I also never developed the habit of baring my soul to him. Or to anyone else since my mother died, except Jan, now and then.

The phone rang again after dinner, as I lay on the living room sofa, reviewing my chapter on flatworms.

"Just got back," Jan panted.

"Sorry I blew up at you," I said.

"Forget it. Low of me to laugh. Did you get things straightened out with Bain?"

"Not exactly," I told her. "Not yet."

"How come?"

I considered lying, but only for a millisecond. "This may be hard to believe, but Ted Steele dragged me out in the hall and started hitting on me."

"My God."

"That's not all," I said. "He called a couple of hours ago, and asked me out for Friday night."

"I don't believe it."

I swallowed hard. "Yes, and I think I accepted."

Silence. To be perfectly truthful, Jan was never one of Ted's major admirers. In fact, she had recently described him as "...conceited, insincere and mentally twisted." Also, as I have related, she saw a bright romantic future for me and Reed. I did not expect her to take my news all that well.

"Wow," Jan finally whispered. "Three hundred girls aching for him and he picks you."

"How about that."

She sounded awfully cheerful. "I know you'll enjoy him."

"You do?"

"Who wouldn't?"

"You're not nauseous or anything?" I asked.

"Not me. Wait till you see my contact lenses."

We talked eyewear for a while and then signed off. Maddie dropped by later that evening to pick up some thread from Mrs. Binder. The minute she walked in, I felt this overpowering urge to tell her every confused detail of my life.

After she left, I lay on my bed close to tears. I *knew* she wanted to listen, stand by me, give advice or anything else she could. The only thing in her way was me.

4.

I walked to school alone, trying to imagine the upcoming wedding. Maddie wanted me in on the arrangements, but I clammed up when she raised the subject. Because it made me uncomfortable, Maddie didn't mention it often. Becoming enthusiastic about the wedding was high on my list of things to do.

But all I could think about as I walked was the mess ahead. Bain, Steele and Hobart in one room. I might, of course, have contracted an instant virus—an approach employed by thousands to dodge less uncomfortable moments than I faced. Sad to say, I could no more fake illness than encourage Reed, embrace my future stepmother or keep my pumping heart calm when Ted Steele whispered through the receiver into my ear.

The school was fairly quiet at eight fifteen, much different from eight forty-five, when I usually arrive. Ted waited for me in the hall and approached me as I came through the stairwell doors.

"Bain-brain and Speedo are both inside." He grinned. His tone implied that *they* were one group and *we* were another. It also made me feel like being with him made *me* special.

That, I think, is real charm.

He placed his hand between my shoulders, walking me down the hall as my heart trip-hammered inches beneath his palm.

Mr. Bain's office is packed with interesting things that he's collected as Social Studies Chairperson: three sets of encyclopedias, shelves of history books, a framed Declaration of Independence, and a parchment Bill of Rights. One wall is entirely covered with pictures of heroes from American history. Thomas Jefferson, Tom Paine, Abe Lincoln, right up through Eleanor Roosevelt, Senator Goldwater, Martin Luther King, Jr. and at least two dozen more.

Reed was gawking at the pictures and Mr. Bain was marking papers at his small wooden desk when Ted and I entered. I, too, looked respectfully at the wallful of faces, hoping it would calm me down. Mr. Bain noted my interest.

"We must be grateful for folks like these." He pointed toward Honest Abe. "Each one searched for the truth and then devoted a life to serving that truth. We all need people like these in our thoughts *and* in our lives. There is strength to be gained from people we can trust and admire, people who have the experience and the will to point the way."

"Hey, okay," Ted piped up.

"Gratified that you agree." Mr. Bain did not look gratified.

"Sure do," Ted persisted. "Heavy dudes and chicks, all of 'em."

Mr. Bain cleared his throat. I had the feeling he would have rather cleared Ted Steele out of his office. He said, "You may have noticed three empty chairs in front of my desk?"

When we were settled into them, I cleared my own throat and said, "Mr. Bain, there's been a mistake."

Three sets of eyes bored into me like laser weapons.

"Hmmmnnn?" he hummed.

"Well, I didn't..." My voice gave out.

"Beg pardon?"

"Sign my name," I blurted.

"On what?" he asked.

"Anything. I didn't volunteer for this. Somebody must have forged my name."

"Oh?" said Mr. Bain.

Reed's mouth lowered like a drawbridge. Ted looked at me curiously. Mr. Bain said, "Who would want to forge your name?"

Possibilities crashed through my mind. Reed, to torment me? Ted, to get next to me? Jan, to have a friend on the court with her? Chubby Arnold? Hyperactive Lisa? I could not imagine.

"Some mental defective," I replied.

After getting the corners of his mouth to behave,

Mr. Bain said, "Whoever it was did the entire class a favor, in my humble opinion."

"Well, thanks..." I murmured.

"Gentlemen, don't you agree?" He nodded at them.

"Huh? Oh...definitely." Reed sounded half-hearted at best.

"Hey, for sure." Ted jerked a fist to his side for emphasis.

"Yes," Bain informed us. "I think Ms. Lang will do nicely."

"Um, that's the thing of it," I said. "I don't want to. I can't."

"Oh?" Bain's forehead creased. His eyes became mournful. "I am deeply sorry to hear it. I looked forward to working with you on this."

Was it a plot? Had Ted and Mr. Bain conspired? Out of the question.

"I'm sorry," I said, "Jan would do it better than me and she'd love the opportunity."

"I suppose," Bain replied. "Still, I think you'd bring something very distinctive to the job."

True, I thought to myself, acute embarrassment leading to a complete and total breakdown.

"Gentlemen, how do you feel about this?"

Ted lit the room with his grin. "I think Sandy's a natural. Not only is she an extra heavy brain, but she's highly respected for not shooting her mouth off like a lot of so-called brainy chicks. In fact, I'd say she's got what you call natural dignity. Right?"

Instead of answering, Mr. Bain turned to Reed.

"Surely you have a thought, Mr. Hobart."

Reed nodded. "If she doesn't have the guts to try it, we should get someone else."

That destroyed all hope of escape. I knew I could no more back out and let Reed think he was right than I could turn into former First Lady Eleanor Roosevelt. Reed's eyes showed *he* knew exactly what he'd done. Mr. Bain sensed it also. His forehead lines smoothed. He relaxed in his chair and waited for someone else to speak.

Ted did. "Watch your mouth, Speedo. Any dude calls Sandy gutless has to deal with me."

"Yeah?" Reed countered.

"Gentlemen, gentlemen," Mr. Bain crooned, so pleased with himself he could taste it. "This really isn't up to us, *is* it?"

He looked at me.

I hated the sight of his face because I knew *he* knew he had me.

"I'll do it."

"Beg pardon?" he asked.

I realized I'd swallowed my big announcement. "I *said* I will *do* it."

"That's wonderful." He smiled.

"Wonderful." I frowned.

"Well, *I'm* sure glad to hear it." Ted's voice poured like honey. I turned to see those ocean-blue eyes gazing right at me. Being looked at like that by a face like that has a reassuring effect.

Reed's expression did not. The way he stared at me and Ted made it clear he wished we'd both evaporate and stay there.

With me in the bag, so to speak, Mr. Bain finally began picking up on the strong emotions flying around his office.

My white-hot fury at being roped in mixed strangely with the tingle Ted's look gave me. But even the longing in Ted's eyes could not quite distract me from the dark disgust with which Reed Hobart now regarded everyone else in the room.

By the time he took all this in, Mr. Bain's usual suave confidence had frayed a bit.

"Now that that's settled," he smiled uncertainly, "shall we get right down to, ah ... business?"

The meeting lasted another fifteen minutes, which only felt like a year and a half. What with Ted gazing and Reed glaring, I quickly dove into my notebook. There I recorded practically every word.

In addition to providing a hideout, taking notes gave me some idea of what went on at the meeting. At the time, I had trouble paying attention. In fact, reading my notes in third period Study Hall was like hearing it all for the first time.

The case, I discovered, was going to be decided on five issues: overall fairness, specific rule-breaking, principles of law, mitigating circumstances, and possible alternative penalties.

The two teams of lawyers were supposed to cover these issues. I was to ask one judge to give a report on each of the issues. Then, all five judges would consider these reports and agree on a final opinion (which the administration could take into account, or just ignore).

Each team of lawyers could call three witnesses. If they wanted to call more they had to get permission from the Chief Justice (me). Each team could examine its witness for fifteen minutes, and the other team could then cross-examine for five minutes—unless the judges granted extensions. Also, there were complicated rules about what kinds of questions the lawyers could ask the witnesses.

My notes show that near the end of the meeting Mr. Bain said, "... this is why I am so pleased to have Ms. Lang as our Chief Justice. I know she will enjoy the confidence of both sides at all times."

I might have smiled when I read that, but remembering how Reed and Ted looked at me paralyzed the necessary muscles.

In the days that followed, the two lawyer teams used class time (and after-school time) to research the facts of the case, interview possible witnesses, try to figure out what "principles of law" were, and decide what they might have to do with people getting suspended over phony program changes. Reed's comic strip became a casualty of the court; he didn't have time while working on the case.

We judges had it easy. All I had to do was hold one meeting to explain the contents of my notes to the other judges. In addition to me and Jan, the panel included:

1. Pete "The Bone" Sweeney: a center on the lacrosse team, smart in math but not much else, okay-looking except for his un-

derweight condition and grunged-out teeth.

2. Mary Jo Fogel: highly regarded drama club star determined to have a movie career without giving up her "values as a human being." Pretty as you'd expect: sky-blue eyes, mile-long lashes, silky brown hair, good figure not hurt at all by daily Jane Fonda workouts.

3. Amy Plutzer: a thin, self-confident person who seemed to be battling one virus or another most of the time.

We held our meeting at my house. Mrs. Binder served us hot apple turnovers and suggested that every last hooligan deserved two weeks in reform school.

After the other three left, Jan said, "See? You're a natural leader. You'll be a great Chief Justice."

It seemed possible.

I *was* feeling quite fine. Why? As we watched lacrosse practice the following Thursday, Jan put it this way, "You're like a different person. You walk different. You carry yourself diff—"

"How?" I asked, knowing what she would tell me.

"More confident. More attractive."

"No kidding?" I said, knowing she wasn't.

"Cross my heart." She did.

I *felt* confident and attractive. Who wouldn't, with Ted Steele flinging eyes every chance he got? And people seemed to look at me differently.

Guys took the time to check me out. Not like they had anything particular in mind. Just like I was someone to check. Was it the way I walked? Well, I didn't pin my shoulders *that* far back—and even if I had, the effect would not have been overwhelming.

Was it the way I dressed? True, I wore a couple of tightish blouses I'd left in the closet before. But again, how much of a difference could that make?

Was it the fact that Ted Steele's hand often rested on my back or at my waist, or that he looked at me so much and winked when we passed in the hall? Very likely. Any girl who interested Ted interested others.

Girls checked me out, too. I was new competition. While socially in the refrigerator, I hadn't been noticed that way. Now I was noticed by every girl with any interest in any guy who even glanced at me.

Of course, most girls believed Ted was only out to win his case. I pretty much believed it myself. So what? The fun of it all had nothing to do with his adoring me. It had to do with the excitement that came with being linked to him. Also, it was the chill I got when he looked at me.

And, there was something else. I felt like I was *going* somewhere. After all those months of feeling depressed, and bored, and irritated with Reed's awkward antics, the pure excitement of motion made me happy.

I did come to one surprising conclusion. In an upside-down way, I seemed to be *using* Ted. So far at least, I hadn't changed my mind about him as a person. I didn't bother telling myself that Ted was misunderstood by girls he wouldn't look at or guys who envied his looks and success. I didn't think about changing him, giving him decent values, showing him how to be good-hearted, like Ron. I liked him for his glamorous image, for what he did and how he did it—not for what he was. I liked him for the fun I was having, not because I really cared.

Not yet, at least. I did consider the risk I was running. If I got too involved, where would I be when the court was over, or when he got bored? Where would I be when he said goodbye or not even that? The risk of a "black hole" replay frightened me a little. But it wasn't enough to scare me away from the pleasant sensation of moving, going somewhere I felt I needed to go.

Toward the end of our talk on Thursday, I looked Jan in the eyes and said, "How come you think it's so great for me to go out with Ted?"

She smiled nervously. "What?"

"How come you didn't tell me to turn him off?" I asked. "After what happened to me after Ron left, aren't you worried now?"

Jan nodded. "Bronto says the same thing."

"Bronto?" I looked away. "You discuss my private life with Bronto?"

She raised both hands in front of her shoulders as though she were being robbed. "Not exactly," she said. "It's just that he asked what was going on and I told him Ted asked you out, and he told me to warn you not to go out with him."

"And?" I prodded.

"I told him you're a big girl and you don't need anyone to warn you about anything."

"Do you really believe that?" I asked.

An uncertain look crossed Jan's face. I kept staring until she let out a big sigh and said, "You want to know why? Because maybe this will get Reed off his butt and make him stop acting like the man who isn't there."

"I don't believe this," I whispered.

She forced a smile. "It might work, Sandrine."

"I don't play those games," I shot back. "I don't need to make Reed jealous. I'm not teasing him and I'm not teasing Ted. Maybe you do that kind of stuff, but I don't."

"No?" She shouted right in my face. "You think you're perfect? Just because you never say what you want? And when you get it you pretend you don't want it anyway, like an innocent little green-eyed saint."

"What's the *matter* with you?" I demanded. Jan had not yelled at me that way in the two years we'd been friends. I didn't know what to do, so I repeated the question several times. She wouldn't answer. We turned our eyes to the field where practice was ending.

After another minute of frosty silence, I got the picture. "I swear I never wanted to be Chief Justice," I said. "I told Mr. Bain to give it to you. I really told him you were the best choice. I couldn't help it. They made me . . ."

Jan heard the catch in my voice and touched my arm. "I know," she mumbled. We started walking together. When we got to her corner she took my wrist in her powerful hand and insisted, "I don't begrudge you, really."

"Okay."

She squeezed gently. "I'm sorry if I gave you bad advice about Ted. I'll be sorry if it doesn't turn out."

I attempted a self-reliant tone. "That won't be your fault."

"One more thing," she said. "This new image of yours isn't only because of Ted. It's not just that you're turning into a willowy beauty."

"No?"

She shook her head. "It's being Chief Justice. You're a major personality now. It's got nothing to do with Ted or anyone else."

I walked home very slowly, using every second to think matters over. Make Reed jealous? Stupid idea. Right out of a sleazy soap. Besides, it would never work. Reed would look down on such a trick just like I would. Not that he could possibly suspect I was using Ted for that. It simply wasn't true. The idea hadn't even occurred to me until Jan mentioned it. Not in so many words. Anyway, I had a right to my own feelings about Ted, *whatever* they were. I didn't owe Reed anything. What had he ever given me? A few kind words in a hallway way back when? So he was a nice person. I never denied that. What I did *not* like was his acting hurt and wounded as though we had some kind of understanding and I was breaking it.

I flashed a picture of Reed standing on one of the docks in the bay. I was moving away, across water. I felt as though we'd been waiting on the dock together until I managed to jump on a boat, and now that I had, I was naturally drifting away from him.

During class the next day, Mr. Bain said, "I'd like to congratulate all of our lawyers and judges on the work they've done so far. Their research has been impressive and I know we'll have a thoroughly fascinating experience in court next week."

Somebody cheered and the class killed a few seconds with applause, which Mr. Bain allowed.

When it died down, he said, "I have one additional announcement in that regard. Our courtroom proceedings will be attended by a slightly larger audience than just this class."

The angel of disaster hovered near.

"The Small Auditorium will be open to all seniors and honor students who are free seventh period and who obtain special passes from their grade advisors. Also, Mrs. Lupavitz's Anthropology class and Mr. Murphy's American History class will attend. Finally, a class of paralegal students from Bambridge Junior College will join us on Tuesday and Friday. I know you will acquit yourselves magnificently."

The angel thudded onto my head. I prayed to it for a serious stomach virus.

5.

Carrots and peas,
Flowers and trees,
Mice in the cheese,
Bad luck in threes.

Mrs. Binder claims her grandmother made that up and it's part of her family heritage. Since she came to us, it's been part of our heritage, too.

It popped into my mind that Friday afternoon when Mr. Bain announced we'd have a monster audience for our Court of Appeals.

That, of course, was Bad Luck Installment Number One. Playing Chief Justice with Jan and Mrs. Binder to back me up in the safety of my living room was one thing. I even toyed with the hope that I *might* avoid disgracing myself before the class. But in front of two *other* classes? Plus any vagrant senior with nothing better to do than haunt the Small Auditorium and enjoy a laugh at blazing pink Sandrine Lang? Add to that a herd of paralegal students from the junior college and this made the black plague seem like *good* luck.

Installment Number Two? My relationship with Reed. In a word, we were not even speaking anymore. I have already described how Ted's blue eyes reached deep inside me and set off ripples. Well, Reed's hate-filled hazel ones reached even deeper, but all they set off was anger! What right did the big gawk have to be mad at *me?* Whenever I could spare the energy, I hated Reed right back.

Bad Luck Installment Number Three? It hadn't happened yet, but I was sure I saw it coming. Ted Steele was certain to get too friendly with me on our first date, and I knew I would respond with some nasty remark destined to halt our little adventure on the spot.

I was talking to Jan outside Mr. Bain's room when Ted kissed the back of my neck and whispered, "See you at the game."

He referred to the big lacrosse clash taking place that afternoon. We were playing McHenry High on our field. Of course, Jan and I planned to attend.

"See?" I said as Ted strutted off and my neck cooled down only slightly. "He's going to be an animal tonight. I know it. I bet he can't remember the last time anyone said 'No' to him, but I'm almost sure I will . . ."

Jan interrupted, "What do you want me to do?"

"Double with us. Tell Bronto. Have him ask Ted."

"Fine," she said. "I'll catch him before he gets to the locker room."

I felt much better. I always got along with Bronto. He's a lot like Jan—strong, straightforward, kind-hearted. And, I knew he had my best interest at heart. With both of them there, at least I'd have some confidence.

I also reminded myself that I'd soon be enjoying Vocabulary Club *without* Reed Hobart around to infuriate me. The coach likes his men to spend forty-five minutes in the locker room before dressing for the game. As Bronto once explained, "Coach believes that sitting together cooped up with nothing to do gets everyone sort of edgy and frustrated, which makes us more awesome on the field."

They hardly ever lost.

I walked up to the third floor relishing the thought of Reed Hobart trapped in the locker room with Ted, Bronto and the rest of them while I escaped from the pressures of daily life into an enjoyable session of Dictionary Dementia in Mrs. Greenwhit's room.

I had, however, miscalculated.

Reed slouched arrogantly by the window overlooking the parking lot as four other regular members waited in their seats. It takes a special kind of high school student to show up late Friday afternoon to play Dictionary Dementia. Like chess club types, only more so. I guess that's me. It's Reed, too, in a funny way.

Needless to say, I was more than a little shocked to see him just then. He curled his lip in an unfriendly greeting. I attempted to ignore him, turning my head and walking more or less calmly to the back.

Mrs. Greenwhit is a slim, high-voiced teacher who takes her work very seriously. She said, "I think a small thank you may be in order. Our star goalkeeper Reed has taken time for our meeting, although he faces McHenry High in little more than an hour. Reed, good luck today, and thanks so much for stopping by."

"Thanks for falling out a window," I whispered to myself.

Dictionary Dementia is one of the world's great pastimes. First, a person picks a really hard dictionary word. Then, other people write down make-believe definitions of that word on scraps of paper. The one who picked the real word writes down the real definition from the dictionary, also on scrap. Then Mrs. Greenwhit reads all the definitions, real *and* phony. The person who picked the dictionary word gets a point every time someone guesses a wrong definition. Each player gets a point for guessing the right definition and a point every time another player guesses his or her phony definition. It sounds a little confusing until you actually play a game.

Mrs. Greenwhit said, "Reed will begin the game because he'll only be here for part of the period. Have you brought us a word, Reed?"

He turned toward the back and before I had time to ignore him again, he flashed a thoroughly evil smile at me.

"Purulent," he said. "P-U-R-U-L-E-N-T." He sounded like a mad professor. "Got that, everyone?"

Mrs. G. wrote the word on the board.

The others nodded, nibbling lips, chewing pencils, fiddling with glasses.

Of course I should have known better, but Reed's posture and smile goaded me into goading him. With the spicy taste of revenge tingling my tongue, I wrote him a little "message" on my square.

Lenny Farokum, the short, excitable Club President, collected our scraps and handed them to Mrs. Greenwhit.

Mrs. Greenwhit read the first definition: "Purulent, afflicted with purulia, a mild disease of the spine." That sounded reasonable, except I'd thought all diseases of the spine were serious.

Heads nodded cautiously. She read the next three slowly, giving us time to digest each one.

"Purulent... a berry-bearing vine of South America. Colloquially, red as a berry. Purulent... late for appointments. Purulent... filled with self-pity, sorrowful, pathetic..."

The last one sounded right. The "p" in purulent seemed to go nicely with the "p" in pity and pathetic. Still, top Dementia players write definitions just that way, to fool you. Sometimes you can tell for sure by looking at the face of the person who picked the word, although technically this is a form of cheating.

Reed's face showed only the hint of a smug smile.

"Purulent." Mrs. Greenwhit paused for a moment, reading the next definition to herself. Mrs. G.'s concerned expression told me she was scrutinizing my scrap. I focused through the corner of my left eye, preparing to enjoy Reed's reaction. Mrs. Greenwhit sighed nervously and continued, "Oafish, self-involved, clumsy, foolish; an utterly forgettable person."

Halfway through it, Reed realized whose definition this was. I certainly did like watching his superior smile disappear as those jaw muscles tensed and those eyes narrowed to slits with the well-aimed insult. Now it was my turn to look self-satisfied. He wouldn't dare turn to glare at me, but I saw him try to steal a sideways glance. I widened my ironic smile.

The rest of the people looked around. It wasn't exactly a normal definition and at least two of them had a rough idea of the personal situation. Not Lenny Farokum.

"What's the last one?" He was breathing hard, caught up in the sheer joy of competition.

Mrs. Greenwhit looked at the next scrap, made an even more uncomfortable face, and read, "Purulent...forming, containing, or discharging pus. Figurative, corrupt, rotten, cheap."

Talk about insults!

I glimpsed Reed grinning hideously at me as my vision went blurry.

The next thing I recall is Mrs. Greenwhit putting five points under Reed's name. (No one had voted for his correct, disgusting definition. Even I hadn't voted for it, although I knew perfectly well which one it was.) Then she put four points under Lenny Farokum's name (he'd invented the "self-pity, sorrowful, pathetic" definition everyone including me voted for), and one point under my name (poor Lenny had been taken in by my little joke on Reed and voted for "...oafish...an utterly forgettable person").

Not that I cared who voted for what.

The words "rotten, corrupt, cheap" chattered inside my skull. *That* was the only reason he'd even shown up—just to let me know what he *really* thought of me. I held back tears, but trembled even harder when Reed grimaced from the doorway and left for his lacrosse game.

Don't get the idea that I actually rooted for McHenry High. But every time they made an attack, I did pray for the ball to bash against Reed's head and bounce into the goal behind him. Of course, I also rooted for Ted to score every time he had the ball, so in that sense I showed complete loyalty to Green Park High.

And, half of my prayers came true. Ted got seven of our twelve goals while Bronto's crashing stick and Reed's reflexes held McHenry High to a pitiful three.

"What's wrong with my casserole?" Mrs. Binder huffed two hours later, when everyone had finished dinner and I still hadn't taken a bite.

"She's got a big date tonight," my father explained. "Sandrine's a little nervous."

"Sandrine's got a date," Bob chanted ten or eleven times.

"Don't be so immature," Brenda scolded.

"I just pray to heaven this one doesn't up and move to St. Louis," Mrs. Binder whispered to me as we cleared the dinner dishes.

My depressions had been brutal on her. Lots of times Mrs. Binder padded into my room as I lay staring at the ceiling. Mostly, she tried to help out by staring along with me.

"I'd probably be better off if this one did move out of town, too," I whispered, sliding a dish into the rack.

I thought about Ron as I waited on the porch. I hadn't had much to do with him until he invited me to the Junior Prom. He was very low-key and fairly nice-looking. People called him "easy-going." We'd been in the same schools since kindergarten, but never in the same class.

I was glad when he asked me to the prom because I was tired of being left out. Not that guys ignored me. But I always acted so shy or sarcastic, that most of the time I wound up alone. I promised myself that Ron would be different. I'd laugh and talk like a normal person. I even asked Jan to make sure I did, which is when she got into the habit of playing romantic coach.

It worked. After the prom, Ron and I stuck together. It wasn't like being in love. It wasn't like Jan and Bronto, for example. Ron was kind, if a

little bit dull, sweet, if extremely predictable, someone who cared and considered me special, and I
had a very nice summer.

That changed in the middle of August, when Ron
broke the news that he was leaving. His father was
offered a partnership in a law firm in St. Louis.
They had to go before school began. As soon as I
heard it, a desperate, frightened emotion took over.
I called it love and told myself I'd go with Ron no
matter what, get a job in a fast-food place in St.
Louis, rent a room, crazy things like that. By the
time he left, I was a wreck. He wrote and phoned,
and I did too, but that tailed off toward the end of
October and he was all I could think about.

Sitting there waiting on my porch, I tried to picture Ron. He had curly brown hair and long thin
hands, but...

I gave up trying to see his features and thought
instead about something that happened last
Thanksgiving. I was having one of my very worst
days. I was so sad I couldn't move. When I wasn't
wanting Ron back, I was cursing Maddie in my
mind and wishing she'd never existed. I'd always
been *sort* of jealous. I didn't like the way she took
up my father's time. I didn't like the way she made
the twins love her. But after Ron left, I really started
to hate her. Sometimes I found myself thinking she'd
made him go. I knew it was pure craziness, but it
felt true just the same.

That Thanksgiving Day I was lying on my bed as

usual. Mrs. Binder had taken a few minutes off from cooking. We had company from my father's family, dinner was in an hour, and she told me she wanted me to be at the table. After I said I would, she stared at the floor.

"Might I have a word with Sandrine?" Maddie stood in the doorway, curvy as a model in her blue silk dress.

Mrs. Binder launched herself from the side of the bed. When she'd gone, Maddie took two steps in the room. I couldn't imagine what she'd say. We never really fought. I'd just get sullen and not talk. Maddie never pressed me to be more pleasant. Neither did Sam J. I guess he knew our little standoff was the best he could hope for. I assumed she'd try something sweet and simple, like "I hope you feel better soon, dear."

But Maddie didn't say anything. After who knows how long, I turned my head toward her. She still didn't speak. I waited a few seconds more and grunted, "What is it?"

Then Maddie said, "I'm here. I'm staying. And that is a fact." And without waiting for an answer, she left the room and went downstairs.

You might think that would have started me crying into my pillow, or dreaming up fantasies of revenge. Instead, a very strange feeling came over me. It was not like I felt great. But something inside relaxed. Fifteen minutes later I was downstairs, more or less grinning at uncles and aunts. Maddie and I have never discussed that incident, but from then on, I stopped hating her.

After Thanksgiving my depressions faded fast. On Christmas Day, I called Ron in St. Louis. We had a nice talk and I hung up wondering what all the fuss had been about.

"Well," I thought as Bronto's Buick wheezed and clanged down the block, "if it isn't one fuss it certainly seems to be another."

The date was pleasant enough. We went to the Brutal Monkeys movie and then to Anthony V.'s for pizza. Ted and Bronto talked a lot about their great game, and Reed's.

Ted behaved like a fine little gentleman. In the back seat, he put his arm around me, and after a while I snuggled against him. He seemed to be all muscles. The Buick pulled up to my house at twelve thirty. As I got out, I heard Ted say, "Don't wait."

The Buick went but I didn't care. I knew by then that Ted would not get too pushy. I asked him in and we went into the kitchen where I boiled water for tea. We sipped it with coffee cake.

"Great flick," he said when I took a seat.

"I know why you're going out with me," I said.

"Yeah?" He looked fascinated. "Why?"

"Because I'm Chief Justice."

"That's right," he said.

"It won't make any difference," I said, eyes on the table. "Whatever goes on with us, it won't make any difference about the Court of Appeals."

"That's not it," he said.

"What's not it?"

"It's not 'cause I want you to favor me." He smiled. "I got interested in you the minute your name went up on the board, but not because I want to get special treatment in Bain's class. It's just that you seemed like a different person. All of a sudden you seemed very important. I don't know how to put it. Very unusual. I sort of noticed you for the first time. And once I did, I was interested."

"Oh?"

He nodded, with his very serious expression. "Don't you think that's possible?"

I didn't answer.

"*Don't* you think it's possible?" He put his hand on mine.

"Don't you want to win?" I asked back.

"Sure. So?"

I dared myself to look into his eyes. "Why do you want to win?" I whispered.

He shrugged, like I'd asked him what color the sky was on a clear, cloudless day.

"It feels good," he said. "What else is there to do?"

The look in his eye when he said it threw some kind of switch in me. I suddenly understood; winning was *all* that really mattered to Ted. He seemed like a wolf or a panther, free to roam and hunt without a worry in the world. There was nothing inside to hold him back. I envied him. I wanted to feel that way.

I didn't know if his line about "noticing me" was true—and I did not care. All I could think of was kissing him. That didn't happen until he left. I opened the door and waited, hoping he would not say goodnight and leave. He smiled and moved closer.

It was a long kiss, and he held me very tight the whole time. Yet the instant our lips met, all excitement vanished. He whistled as he walked to the sidewalk, but I had not felt a thing. And I looked at the ceiling until three in the morning trying to figure out why.

6.

"**I**'ve had a very romantic past."

I exaggerated slightly describing the previous summer with Ron.

Spring sunshine brightened our Saturday afternoon as I pulled weeds from my tulip patch and Jan watched from a white, wrought iron backyard chair, helpfully pointing out little weeds I might otherwise overlook.

"I remember," Jan replied. She should have. Most of our more or less romantic times took place in the back of Bronto's Buick.

"So what's wrong?" I asked.

"Nothing's wrong," she assured me.

"No?" I tugged at a big nasty one. "Then how come I didn't feel anything when he kissed me? He's only the best-looking specimen I've ever seen close up and he's been giving me goose bumps with his eyes all week."

Jan considered this thought and concluded, "You never can tell."

"Wonderful. I think I may have one of those problems the old lady doctor talks about at two in the morning on channel 3."

"You watch Dr. Getweiler, too?" Jan looked amazed.

"Only when I can't sleep. Maybe I suffer from polar lips." I stopped weeding. "What do you think?"

She shrugged.

I suddenly knew what was on Jan's mind and pointed my four-pronged gardening tool at her.

"*You* think I froze on Ted because I'm afraid he's just *using* me. You think that's why I didn't like kissing him."

She shrugged again.

"Is that it?" I demanded.

"How should I know?"

"But do you think it? Believe it? Suspect it?"

"Suspect what?"

I fixed her with a sharp glance. "Do you think Ted's just using me?"

She avoided the issue by pointing out a green speck of weed near my sneaker.

"*Do* you?" I brought the gardening tool to hurling position behind my head.

She sighed. "You want the honest truth?"

That terrified me, but I said, "Yes. Immediately."

Jan said, "Maybe he's using you."

I collapsed onto the grass.

□ □ □

She went on, "That *is* what most people think. But who knows, maybe he *was* being honest when he said that baloney about noticing you for the first time. Why? You think you could get hurt?"

"I don't think so. But I sure am curious. Don't you think he was being even slightly honest?" I got to my knees and looked up at her.

"Personally, I don't." Jan forced a smile. "But it's a possibility. A ting like dot izz hard to zay for suuure." She closed one eye and raised her finger in a so-so imitation of Dr. Luba Getweiler.

While my busy hands spent the rest of Saturday and most of Sunday planting flowers and early vegetables, my overactive mind passed the time pondering my unenthusiastic response to Ted's expert embrace, the likelihood that Ted might really have fallen in love with me, and the depths of my dislike for the overgrown boob of a goalkeeping buffoon who had all but described me in front of fellow Vocabulary Club members as "corrupt, rotten and cheap."

Sunday night I got out my dictionary. It wasn't the same one Reed had used, so the definition wasn't word for word. But "purulent" meant exactly what Reed said it did. I didn't know whether to detest him more or less because of that.

At school Monday, Ted blew kisses when we passed, winked, and once came over to touch my cheek. But just before the first court session, he stopped me outside the Small Auditorium.

"Listen," Ted said, "maybe we ought to cool it a little until the court is over next week."

"Cool what?"

"Well, not the way we *feel* about each other, of course." He whispered intensely. "But showing it in public. It might not look too good considering the court and all. People might get the wrong impression."

I nodded.

He continued. "So we'll just go on like nothing's happening, and next weekend we'll make it up to each other, right?"

"Right," I replied.

That was all I needed. On top of facing my class, Mrs. Lupavitz's anthropologists, Mr. Murphy's historians, roving bands of seniors, honor students, and paralegal students, I now had to worry about what Ted Steele might be up to.

Which is exactly what I did as Mr. Bain introduced the proceedings and the two Chief Attorneys gave their five-minute opening statements.

Strangely enough, that distraction helped. Although feverish thoughts of Ted kept my mind off the proceedings, they also kept it off the audience. When it came time for me to ask Reed to present his first witness, I'd already spent twenty minutes on public display at the center of the judges' table in front of the Small Auditorium—too lost in thought to be nervous, embarrassed or scared.

As a result, I never even blushed.

I will not go into the details of the four-day court proceedings, but generally speaking, it went well. Everyone followed the rules and pretty much avoided showing off. The audience kept more or less quiet, and I did not have to make many hard decisions on which questions to allow.

My main problem was looking at the two Chief Attorneys, especially when they were looking at me. By the end of the first day, all I could see were those two pairs of penetrating eyes. Not that anyone noticed my problem. In fact, the audience seemed caught up in the case itself.

Here are some of the highlights according to the five areas Mr. Bain told the lawyers to address:

1. Overall fairness: Would a reasonable person consider what the administration did as fair?

2. Specific rule-breaking: Did the culprits really break any rules? If they did, did they know it?

3. Principles of law: Such as, do people have to have a fair hearing before they can be found guilty?

4. Mitigating circumstances: Were the culprits forced to do what they did? Example: If you are starving, that is a mitigating circumstance for stealing food.

5. Possible alternative penalties: Could the administration have handed out a more appropriate one?

Each team could call witnesses for fifteen minutes each. Then the other team could cross-examine for five minutes (which meant about one or two questions) unless the judges gave more time. Because we only had four periods to wrap things up, it always seemed like we were running out of time, so I didn't give much extra time to anyone—not even when Ted batted those heart-melting blues at me, or Reed tried to scare me with ferocious stares.

Ted's defense team made a *very* strong, if not too exciting, case on the issue of specific rule-breaking. Ted called Dean Benoit who gave a dramatic reading of Board of Education rules for making program changes. He followed that with paragraphs from the school disciplinary code.

Dean Benoit had the time of his life. He spoke in a deep, cultured voice from behind his huge shaggy moustache. The moustache makes his appearance. Without the thing, he'd look very ordinary in a small, balding way.

Reed cross-examined Dean Benoit. At one point, Reed said, "Those rules talk about 'voluntary infractions.' What does this mean?"

"It means rules that are being broken by people who know what they are doing, or should know what they are doing," the dean declared.

"I see. How many of the suspended people *knew*

they were breaking the rules when they used this stamp?"

"All, I assume," boomed Dean Benoit.

"Assume?" Reed looked horrified. "You merely *assume* they broke the rules on purpose? Did you at least ask them?"

"Of course," answered Dean Benoit, sounding slightly ruffled. "I personally discussed the incident with them and they did not deny full understanding of what they had done. None of them did."

"Did you discuss the incident with *all* of the suspended students?"

"About half, I think. Some did not come to the meetings I arranged. They simply accepted their suspensions without protest."

Reed said, "Would it surprise you to learn that at least *one* student claims he believed the procedure was completely all right because a friend of his *told* him so?"

"I was not aware of that—" Dean Benoit sounded irritated now—"but as long as this student actually *did* it, the rule-breaking took place, and the suspension applies."

"You see no difference between a voluntary rule-breaker and an innocent victim of bad advice?"

"No," Dean Benoit huffed.

Reed then read a statement signed by Omar Galindez saying that a friend (whom he would not name) told him the procedure was okay. Omar also stated that he did not explain this to Dean Benoit because he did not want to go through the "ordeal" of a meeting. Also, it never occurred to Omar that what he thought at the time would make any difference, anyway. Time ran out just as Reed finished his cross-examination of Dean Benoit.

Reed's team introduced the next witness. Surprisingly, they let Richie Green do the questioning. Richie seemed terribly nervous and I hoped he wouldn't revert to his stuttering ways. He stalled and stalled, playing with his three-by-five note cards, going back to the table, whispering with Sheila Dufay. Just when he looked ready to start, someone at Ted Steele's table made an impatient noise.

I shot a stern glance at them. Richie hesitated again and turned toward Reed, who crossed his eyes, of all things. That struck me as extremely bizarre, but it did the trick. Wiping the smile from his face, Richie stepped forward to greet his witness, the highly respected Bronto Gould, all-around senior and two-day suspension victim.

Slowly and confidently, Richie asked Bronto to kindly explain what happened when he tried to change from Badminton to Conversational French. Being a super jock, the last thing Bronto needed was extra gym credits. He got stuck in Badminton because his grade supervisor or the school computer or someone else goofed. Mistakes like that happen from time to time, Bronto said. Then he started reeling off examples.

"I object." Ted jumped up from his first-row seat. "That's hearsay evidence."

"I will allow the testimony," I said. "Since this point is important, Mr. Gould may continue. The court will have to decide if his evidence is useful."

"I object too," griped chubby Arnold Playfield, making his only contribution of the entire court. "One judge is a lacrosse player and another one is Bronto's old lady. Almost half this court has to believe his testimony's useful no matter *what* he says."

Playfield seemed thrilled with himself until vivacious volleyballer Lisa Hooper snapped, "Button your face, Arnold."

By the time Bronto finished, everyone had a vivid picture of what most people already knew: changing your program card, even for the best possible reasons, could cost you hours of waiting in the guidance office and land you in your new class a week late with five assignments to make up on top of your regular work.

Ted and Lisa had a brief argument about who was going to cross-examine Bronto. Ted began by making a speech about how "patience and obedience help the world go 'round." I had to suggest he ask the witness some questions. He thanked the court for correcting him and asked whether Bronto believed it was a good idea for students to take the law into their own hands just because they didn't like the way the system worked.

"Sometimes," Bronto said.

That set off a minor cheering epidemic. I smacked the judges' table with a little wood gavel Mr. Bain had given me. The place quieted right down. Mr.

Bain smiled so widely I thought the front row would fall into his mouth.

On the issue of principles of law, Ivy League scholarship collector Sheila Dufay examined Mr. Bain about the Bill of Rights. It sounded like "Meet the Geniuses" on public television. Mr. Bain testified that American justice gives accused persons the right to hear the evidence against them, and to confront their accusers—which all the suspended people did not get to do.

Ted cross-examined. He got Mr. Bain to admit that according to the Supreme Court, schools did not have to follow the Bill of Rights exactly. Ted liked Mr. Bain so much he kept him up there the next day as his own witness. Mr. Bain went on to explain that schools, prisons, the armed forces, and a few other institutions have to maintain order under special circumstances, so they are allowed to cut down on the Bill of Rights here and there.

Reed cross-examined. He got Mr. Bain to say that the more rights people have, the better.

"I would argue the notion," Bain nodded, "that whenever possible, accused persons should enjoy all the rights described in the Bill of Rights."

Reed threw me a tiny smile which, if I hadn't been so repelled by the sight of him, might have been slightly charming.

Both teams didn't get around to overall fairness and possible alternative penalties until their final statements Thursday.

Reed began his written speech by saying, "This is a difficult case. Our side does not pretend that it's simple. On one hand, rules were broken and we recognize that at least some people probably knew they were breaking rules when they did it. But we also claim that some people may *not* have understood the situation completely. Take the case of Omar Galindez. He was told by a trusted friend that this was a new procedure which the administration approved. Other people may also have believed that. For this reason, we demand that all suspensions be revoked until each one is reviewed on a case-by-case basis.

"Second, we point out that there are times when rules and even laws must be broken. For example, some countries are ruled by totalitarian governments. In such countries the law is used to beat down and oppress the people. In such countries breaking the laws may be necessary and even heroic, rather than criminal."

Some of the paralegal students clapped, but I stopped them with a hit of the gavel. Reed smiled. "I do not suggest that Dean Benoit is a dictator." Giggles sprouted here and there. "But I do suggest that the administration has made a serious mistake. And because of that mistake, it should change the penalties which its own mistake *caused*. What *was* that mistake?"

Reed waited to be sure everyone ached for the answer. He turned to me with the look of a kid who has tied his shoes for the first time. He had reason to be proud. I thought he'd put together a very good case, considering the facts. He had emphasized overall fairness and mitigating circumstances to make as little as possible of Ted's solid issue—rules and regulations. Now, two hundred people hung on his next words.

He ended their suspense by explaining which "serious mistake" he meant. It was, of course, the terrible system for making program changes. This, Reed claimed, was reason enough for Dean Benoit to reconsider his decision to suspend the fifty-three students. And, to avoid wasting even more time with case-by-case reviews, Reed's team suggested cancelling all the suspensions and replacing them with simple letters of reprimand, which would not go in anyone's permanent record.

This time it took a little longer for me to control the applause. As I banged my gavel, I pictured Reed raising his stick to the net's upper corner, attempting a brilliant, impossible save, missing the ball by a fraction of an inch.

Ted's closing statement was the last item on the court's agenda. Unlike Reed, who talked to the whole audience and all of the judges, Ted gave his speech mostly to me. It boiled down to this: People will always break rules—but when they do, they must be prepared to pay the price if they get caught. Even great Americans who broke bad laws because they wanted to change them did not complain about going to jail. In fact, they considered it an honor. That's how the rule of law is protected.

So, if the culprits believed they did right, they should just hope their sacrifice will help improve program-changing procedures for the generations to come. And if they believed they did wrong, they should admit that the penalties could have been worse.

No cheering followed, but you could see that some people got his point.

After Ted sat down, Mr. Bain walked up to the stage and congratulated all the participants. Then he congratulated the audience for keeping their mouths shut so nicely. He invited them to cheer and applaud for themselves, which they did.

Just as I was congratulating myself for getting through the week without veering anywhere near the breakdown I'd expected, I heard Mr. Bain say, "I think we should now recognize the extraordinary contribution of our Chief Justice, Sandrine Lang, who ran the court for us with care, command and courtesy."

The blush I'd managed to avoid all week turned me tomato-red in two seconds. Ted leaped to his feet pounding both hands over his head. Reed Hobart eyed me maliciously, stood, clapped his huge paws once, and sat down. My flaming ears rang as the gruesome ovation continued.

7.

Fifteen minutes later, we judges had a meeting with Mr. Bain in his classroom. He asked whether we'd discussed the case among ourselves during the week. As requested, Jan and I had not discussed it even with each other. Jan had raised the subject several times. I had told her I wanted to follow the case without being influenced by her brilliant mind. Jan gave me long, ironic looks, but finally promised she wouldn't discuss it with anyone else except Bronto. "Just to keep up appearances," she added, winking slyly.

The others said they hadn't discussed it either. Maybe not. But sitting next to them all week gave me some idea of how they felt. Pete Sweeney and Jan were against the administration one hundred percent. Mary Jo Fogel started out that way, but seemed less convinced as the week went on. Amy Plutzer's feelings remained mysterious behind sniffles, red eyes, and other cold symptoms.

Mr. Bain explained once again that we should either recommend overturning Dean Benoit's decision, and suggest another remedy, or uphold the administration's position.

Mr. Bain said, "Overturn only if you feel the administration made a clear and serious mistake, failed to do their job right as described by the Board of Education rules."

We assured him we would.

"Sandrine," he said as the others got up, "can you give me just a few minutes more?"

Jan and I planned to watch practice as we had every day that week. I asked her to wait for me at the field.

"I'm sorry if I embarrassed you with my closing remark," Mr. Bain said when we were alone. He stretched behind his desk. I fidgeted in a first-row seat. "I thought you were *past* embarrassment." He tapped the desk with a pencil.

I wanted to watch Ted, Reed, Bronto and the others dash around in shorts, wave their sticks, run into each other.

"How'd you know I was embarrassed?" I asked. "Because I *blushed?*"

Mr. Bain seemed halfway embarrassed himself. "Perhaps just the tiniest bit. Have you figured out who forged your name on the scrap sheet?"

"No," I said. "but whoever did it had better hope I *never* find out."

"Don't you think it's turned out well?" He narrowed his eyes over the tops of his horn-rims.

"I suppose."

He paused. "Then perhaps you'd be inclined to forgive whomever did it?"

"Not on my deathbed."

"I see." He nodded.

I tried to look impatient. I didn't want to miss calisthenics.

"On a personal level, Sandrine, I'm very grateful for the way you rose to the challenge. I knew from the beginning that the success of my little experiment would depend largely on the Chief Justice. That's where the tone and seriousness of the process had to be reflected and exemplified—"

Click.

A 200-watt light bulb flooded my brian with light. He peered nervously over the glasses.

I said, "*You* forged my name, *didn't* you?"

"I'm afraid so."

I wasn't sure exactly how to feel. I knew I should resent getting double-crossed. But I couldn't imagine him wanting to hurt me. Part of me tried to be furious. But another part felt very nice, flattered in fact. Just what I needed—another squirming batch of mixed emotions.

"Can I go now?" I asked.

He nodded. When I got to the door, he said, "Are you angry?"

"I'm not sure," I said. "I really can't tell."

□ □ □

"Pssst." I looked around, but didn't see anyone in the narrow basement hall leading toward the playing field. I checked back around the corner I'd just turned. Nobody there. I walked on, pretty sure that someone was hiding in the little alcove just before the door which opens onto the field.

"Glad I caught you." Ted smiled, emerging from the space all decked out in shoulder-and-arm pads, gloves, shorts, smelly green sweatshirt, cleats and shin guards, holding his helmet and stick under one yummy arm.

"Are you hiding?" I asked.

"Hey, of course not. Just waiting to have a private chat with you. Jan said you were on your way."

I looked at him carefully. "Shouldn't you be doing jumping jacks or something?"

"That's a matter of opinion. I think it's more important for us to have a chat."

"Okay," I said, unable to guess what was coming.

"It's about the court. About your decision." He looked down at me from the extra inch and a half his cleats gave him. "I just want you to know that whatever you do is fine with me. I know you'll give a fair decision according to your conscience."

"You're right," I said. "I will."

He nodded. "The only thing is, I'm afraid you might be in kind of a difficult position here."

"Why?" I asked.

Now this is not easy to explain. But just at that moment, his eyes changed. They didn't turn a different color or grow or shrink, but they became electric. I definitely felt current passing between us.

"Look," he said softly, intensely, "you know I don't want any favors from you. I said that all along. Whatever happens, it won't change my feelings for you. I'll feel the same. I don't want you even thinking about that."

I wouldn't be surprised if getting hypnotized feels like I did then. I heard his words but I didn't. Mainly I sensed his voice echoing from the walls and swirling around my head.

"You *know* I want you to do what's right." His voice became a deep whisper. "And I know you'd never do anything else, not for me or any other guy. I know you'll follow your conscience no matter what."

By that time, my heartbeat was up to its old tricks. I wondered how I'd managed my imitation of cold rain when he kissed me Friday night.

"But I have to admit, I'm just a little worried about another problem," he said.

I knew I wouldn't have to ask. I heard one of his gloves hit the floor. He touched my face with two fingers, stroking my cheek very gently, and said, "A person like you cares about her conscience most of all. I know that. I know it because I've got a conscience too. People don't understand that about me, but I do have one. Maybe not as strong a conscience as yours, but I've got one, so I understand. And next to your conscience, I know you care about what people think. Not how you look or who you go out with, or anything superficial like that, but how honest you are. Like I said in Bain's office, your integrity?"

He waited for an answer. I fought an urge to catch his fingers and press them to my face. Instead, I gave a little nod to show I was listening.

"Now, even though we've sort of kept our feelings for each other under control, a lot of people know how it is between us, right?"

I nodded again.

"So it seems to me that without even thinking it, like unconsciously, if you know what I mean, you might feel like you need to bend over backwards the other way, just to prove that you're *not* favoring me. I wouldn't even blame you if you did."

"Did what?" I asked, trying to answer questions of my own without getting lost in the blue of his eyes and the swirl of his whirring whisper.

"You know," he said, "if you favored the other side just to make sure you weren't favoring me because of how we feel about each other. I really think that's the main danger, the thing to watch out for most. So that's all I have to say. Just be sure you don't go overboard in the other direction, okay? 'Cause that wouldn't be fair either, would it?"

He began to inch his face closer. I was so curious that my lips trembled. I closed my eyes.

"Welcome to sleaze city."

Gasping with horror and feeling my eyelids fly open like window shades, I saw Reed Hobart stand in the doorway resembling a scarecrow from outer space, goalie pad on his chest and stomach, face-protector helmet on his head, long arms and legs framed by bright sunlight.

Off came the helmet.

"Having a little *conference?*" he snarled down at us.

"Back off, dirtbag," Ted barked. "What'd you do? Follow me?"

"Like garbage to the dump."

"Who's garbage?" Ted growled.

"Who isn't?" Reed hissed.

Ted's other glove dropped. He bunched a fist in front of his face. "How'd you like to *eat* some garbage?"

"How'd you like me to chew you up and spit you out?" Reed moved from the doorway into the hall, toward us.

They started shoving. Ted threw a punch that caught Reed in the chest protector. Reed bounced one off the side of Ted's head. The cleats couldn't get much traction on the cement floor so they quickly went down, grabbing each other's shirts, rolling back and forth, crashing from one wall to the other, cursing, grunting, pulling, thrashing.

It really was disgusting. I know some people enjoy watching that kind of thing, but I don't. The fact that I seemed to be the cause of it made matters worse. And even worse than that, I couldn't figure out what to do about it.

First I tried yelling, like I do when the twins get

physical. "You stop that right..." It sounded so ridiculous I failed to finish the sentence.

Next, I tried to separate them by bending over and tugging their shirts. While I did, I prayed for Jan to show up. She'd been lifting weights with Bronto for over a year, and was stronger than lots of guys. With her at my side I might have had a chance. But they were rolling around so fast that all I managed to do was get punched in the foot, and banged on the knee by somebody's big, muddy cleats.

After that, I decided to leave and let them tear each other to shreds. But something told me that wasn't right, either.

For a few seconds I thought about running outside and calling for help, but the last thing I wanted was a crowd of people witnessing this mess.

Finally, I tried to stop the fight by distracting the fighters. I kicked both of them as hard as I could, anywhere except the face, first one then the other. If I'd had a few more seconds, I'm sure that would have worked.

However, what actually stopped the fight was Bronto sticking his big square face through the door and then reaching down like a human earth mover to push Ted off Reed. When Ted tried to jump back on Reed, Bronto flung him against a wall. After that, Ted turned all his attention to breathing.

Reed was already too out of breath to continue fighting, even if he was stupid enough to think he could get past Bronto.

Also out of breath, I stood there listening as Bronto squelched further debate by informing Ted and Reed that the fight had never happened. They nodded. Then he suggested they shake hands, noting that if they didn't shake hands with each other, they'd have to shake hands with him, which would be worse. They took the easy way out.

Bronto looked down at me. "It never happened, right?" I nodded up at him.

Reed looked away as he passed.

Ted left last. "Hey," he said smiling, "all's fair in love and war, right babe? See you tomorrow, Sandy."

I stood there pretty much drained for a minute or so. When Jan finally turned up I was studying a wall.

"They had a fight, didn't they?" she squealed.

I nodded.

"That is so *exciting!*" She clasped her hands like a little kid.

"We're supposed to pretend it never happened," I told her. "Bronto wants to protect team morale or something."

"They didn't *hurt* each other, did they?" she asked, suddenly serious.

"Nah. Just rolled around and cursed a lot."

"Tell me all about it. How did it start?"

"It's stupid," I said.

"Tell me. Come on."

I knew telling her would be easier than arguing, so I said, "I was just talking to Ted, and Reed showed up and they started shoving each other."

"*Just* talking to Ted?" Jan asked.

"Yes. Just talking." It was true, if only by a split second.

"What were you talking about?"

I said, "About the opinion we will write tonight. He told me he knows I'll give an honest opinion, and that's all he expects."

"That's *all* he said?"

I nodded. "That's all."

She moved her head as though seeing me from different angles gave her a better look at the truth. "Are you absolutely *sure* he didn't try to change your mind? Even a little?"

I figured that if I told Jan about the last part of our conversation, where Ted asked me not to bend over backwards *against* him, she'd definitely think he was trying to influence my opinion. And that might influence *her* opinion even more against the administration than it already was. My idea at the time was to keep these personal emotions out of it as much as possible.

"No," I told her firmly, "Ted did not try to influence me. He told me to just follow my conscience."

Her face brightened. "Wow," she said.

"Wow what?" I asked.

"It looks to me like you've got *both* of 'em nuts over you."

"I'm going home now," I said.

We stopped by the field for Jan to pick up her books.

"I really don't know what to do," I told her as we neared the corner where we split up.

"About what?"

"About writing the opinion," I said. "I'm starting to worry that maybe I can't trust myself to be fair. It's not that I *want* to favor anyone. But the two of them are in my head now. I don't even know how I feel about them, let alone how my emotions are going to influence me."

"Say again?" Jan's thumb and forefinger held her smooth, pretty chin.

"I mean, my unconscious mind," I said. "It can change the way you think without your even knowing it. You remember."

"Of course I do," Jan confirmed. "I sat next to you in Theories of the Mind, didn't I? But you're wasting your time."

"Yeah?"

Jan sighed as though it were the most obvious thing in the world. "No matter *what* your unconscious mind says, you have to vote the same way everyone else does."

"I do?"

"Of course. We all have to vote against the administration. Didn't you listen to Reed?" She lectured me like a first-grader. "You, me and Pete have a majority right off the bat. I'm sure the other two will make it unanimous, but even if they don't, who cares? The majority rules. That's it. Forget your unconscious mind."

"I don't know about that," I said.

Jan's eyes narrowed. "Don't know about what?"

"Voting that way. Automatically."

Her mouth twitched. "Hey, we have to stick together. We have to stick up for the fifty-three students, including your friend and mine, Bronto Gould."

"What does Bronto say?" I asked.

"He doesn't care what happens because he's already accepted in Syracuse with his scholarship."

"So?" I reasoned. "If he doesn't care, why should you?"

"It's the principle of the thing. There is a right and a wrong, Sandrine. The administration is wrong and the students are right, and that's been true since history began."

"I don't know," I said.

Jan replied, "You have been acting a little funny lately. Maybe all this excitement *is* affecting your mind."

I spoke very calmly. "Are you telling me that from the first time you volunteered to get on this court, you planned to vote against the administration no matter what the evidence showed, or what Mr. Bain said, or anything else?"

"Of course." Jan looked puzzled. "Didn't you?"

I shook my head.

"Oh, boy." She whistled through her teeth.

The corner was chilly that afternoon, but we stood there a long time until Jan broke the painful silence.

"Sandrine, the point of all this is loyalty. Fifty-three students got suspended for no good reason. It goes on their record. Bronto may not care personally, but some of the others do. And we are there to get them off the hook. And if we can't do that, we are there to make the administration look stupid for suspending them. What do you think is going on here?"

"I don't know," I said. "Do you think that's what Mr. Bain expects?"

Jan took a deep breath and patiently tried again. "Everyone in the world has a different job. Benoit's job is to be an administrator and pretend he's running the school. Fine. That's his career. Bain's job is to teach us about law and democracy and similar things, correct? So he cooks up hot projects like the Court of Appeals, and he gets off on that. We are *students*. Our job is to stick together and make sure nobody, including Bain or Benoit, gets over on our friends. Loyalty. Nothing more, nothing less."

"I'm not so sure," I said.

Jan's contacts gleamed in the reddening sunlight. *"What* are you not sure about?"

"Whether loyalty to the students is the only thing."

"What *else* could there *be?*" Jan demanded.

"We told Bain we'd follow the rules and *then* decide according to the evidence. That's the point of the court, isn't it? That's what we said we'd do, right?"

"Of course we did," Jan snapped, her patience

wearing thin. "If we didn't agree to it, we couldn't be *on* the court."

"But I meant it when I agreed. I didn't think of it that way, the way you did."

"So?" She seemed ready to blow up.

I paused to be sure I had my thoughts clearly in mind. "So I feel like I have to do what I said I'd do. I said I'd make up my mind according to the rules and the evidence."

Jan seemed even angrier than when she'd called me a green-eyed saint. Her anger scared me. I thought I might lose her if I kept pushing my point. "I gave my word," I said weakly.

She practically roared in my face. "Don't tell me you're in love with old Bain, too! Okay, look at it this way. What would *he* do if he were fifty years younger? He'd do what I'm telling *you* to do. Bain's okay. He knows right from wrong. You want to be Bain's good little girl? Then just think what *he'd* do if he were a student and not a teacher."

I snapped, "You're getting a little witchy, Jan."

"And you are getting a little nuts."

Part of me agreed with her. Here I was talking about giving my word to Mr. Bain after he'd double-crossed me in the first place. It sounds nutty now and it sounded nutty then, but it did not *feel* nutty.

"I have to keep my word," I repeated.

Jan waved her finger in my face. "I was right all along. It's just a matter of loyalty. And I can see now that *you* are only loyal to *yourself*." She turned, but then whipped her head around to spit out a final thought. "You and Ted Steele belong together, lady."

She walked to her house without turning again.

I felt myself dividing in half like a little one-celled creature. One half knew exactly how she felt and wanted to stay on her good side by voting her way. And that wasn't all. Something in me rooted for Reed despite his attitude. I didn't agree with what Benoit did and I thought it was a shame about the suspensions. In addition to which, I did *not* want people considering me a back-stabbing creep.

Yet the other half of me would not give in. It clung to that little sentence "I gave my word" like it was the law. I imagined Jan telling her brothers I had some nerve— pretending my "word" was more important than fifty-three suspensions.

I thought about it all the way home, trying to find a way out. Neither side of me would budge, yet neither could make the other give in. Most infuriating of all, I had a very strong feeling that the answer was sitting right under my nose.

8.

I was certainly on the shaky side when I got home to find Mrs. Binder waiting for me in the living room.

She grabbed my hand, hauled me into the kitchen, sat me down at the table, and darted into her room. Five minutes later she came out wearing a black sequined dress that made her look like a chandelier.

"Well?" she asked.

"Doesn't she look *gorgeous?*" Brenda said from the back door, Bob looking over her shoulder.

I nodded. "Beautiful. Where'd you get it?"

She whirled again. "My kids gave it to me for my thirty-third wedding anniversary. Eight years ago and I haven't put on a pound since."

She turned to prove it.

"Amazing," I agreed.

"I want to show Maddie," Mrs. B. announced. "I'm wearing it to the wedding if she approves."

"She will. You'll steal the show."

"Good gracious, I hope not."

Bob and Brenda tumbled inside, demanding snacks. I cut up oranges while Mrs. Binder changed into her yellow smock.

"I'll put it on later," she puffed. "It sure is an effort, though."

"What is?"

"Fitting myself in. What are *you* going to wear?"

I said, "The green silk, I guess." I'd worn it once, to the junior prom.

She made a disgusted face.

"What's wrong with that?" I asked.

"You can't go in an old dress. I never heard of such an idea. Have Maddie take you to buy a new one."

I should have said, "Good suggestion," or "I'll ask at dinner." Instead, I gave her an angry look and stomped out of the kitchen with Bob and Brenda staring after me.

Maddie and my father were a few minutes late, so Mrs. Binder was upset at them, too. She believes that her garlic and mustard pork roast "loses most of its magic" when it stands twenty minutes or more.

I tried to cheer her up by telling everyone at the table they had a big treat in store, and that Mrs. Binder would never look the same to them.

"She's ravishing," Brenda commented during the mid-dinner fashion display.

"You're *ravishing*," Bob mimicked, giggling fiendishly when Brenda missed three straight punches.

My father asked, "How was your last day of court?"

"It had its moments," I said, helping myself to spinach salad.

"Such as?" He bit a chunk of pork and grinned ecstatically for Mrs. Binder's benefit.

Sam J.'s seemingly innocent question had an odd effect on me. My brain began to feel like a busy intersection, pell-mell rush hour traffic growing crazier each second. I watched my words, like runaway cars, speed through my mind and out of my mouth with no one to stop them or even slow them down.

"Just a few things," were the first to shoot out. "Mr. Bain got the whole auditorium to applaud for my great job as Chief Justice and I almost had a blood pressure crisis on the spot. Then I got Mr. Bain to admit he picked me for the job and let me think someone else forged my name on a scrap sheet. He made me a judge under false pretenses and got me to promise that I would follow the rules of the court, so I think I'll report him—"

My father opened his mouth to speak, but Maddie stopped him with her eyes.

I continued. "And of course there's this guy I went out with Friday night..."

"Woo, woo," hooted Bob.

"Shush!" threatened Sam.

"He's one of the lawyers in the case and he surprised me in the hall and got me to swear I wouldn't bend over backwards to decide the case against him to prove how honest I am. And then the other lawyer, who is about the skeeviest guy I *ever* met except I thought I liked him once upon a time, which is ancient history, came along and the two of them started fighting in their lacrosse outfits which made me sick until Bronto Gould just happened to come along and attack them both."

"Uh-oh," my father said.

"Woo, woo!" shouted Bob.

Maddie watched me blink tears away.

"And after that, I lost my best friend in the world because she thinks I'm nothing but a low-life traitor. We have different opinions on how the judges should act, and loyalty to fellow students, and so forth. And the worst thing is, I don't *know* who's right or wrong, and even if I did, I don't know if I should follow the rules or ignore all the evidence and just vote against the administration or keep my word to Mr. Bain, or worry about Jan, or Reed, or Ted. I can't even think straight anymore and I *know* I'll be a babbling idiot when I have to work on the decision with the other judges."

I caught my breath and then slowed down a little. "And the worst part of all is, we're having our meeting tonight."

"I know," my father said. "I bought the cookies."

I nodded miserably, far too emotional to realize that I was telling everyone my personal business, right in front of the children.

"I'm all messed up," I sighed.

"Sounds complicated," Sam J. agreed.

"Jan thinks the court is a joke," I went on. "She says we have to vote automatically for the students, and maybe she's right. If I *did* agree with her maybe I wouldn't want to be friends with a low-life traitor, either, but I can't pretend I think she's right if I don't. And I can't even *think* of favoring Ted, who is only the cutest guy in the state and it's not every day someone who looks like a major movie star falls all over you, right?"

My father tried a smile. "I guess not," he said.

"But on the other hand, I can't bend over backwards to influence the court *against* Ted and *for* Reed just to show the world how honest I am. That would be just as unfair even if I *was* trying my best to do the right thing. Besides which, being Chief Justice wasn't even my idea in the first place and that's just what Mr. Bain *deserves* for being such a sneaky two-face, right?"

"Well," my father said, "it's hard to be sure."

That response triggered another unexpected reaction in me. The high-speed traffic jam froze. As calm replaced the hubbub between my ears, an idea drifted into view like a cloud above the suspended commotion.

"I know what to do," I said.

Relief blossomed across my father's face. "What?"

"Not vote," I declared.

"That's a sin." Mrs. Binder waved our bright red

teapot from the kitchen door.

"Not for president," I told her. "For whether to overturn the school administration."

That seemed to mortify Mrs. B. even more, but she let me complete my thought.

"I'll just say I can't make up my mind and I'll be like a referee when the judges come over here to vote. I'll help them decide what they think and I'll help them put their opinions into words. But I won't say what I think. I won't express a single opinion of my own. It doesn't make any difference anyway. They've all made their minds up. So why should I even go to the trouble, especially when everyone's going to assume that I thought whatever I did think for the wrong reason, no matter *what* I actually do think or say. I swear it makes me sick and that's exactly what I will do."

"What?" Bob asked.

"Not vote." I rapped the table, startling him.

"Good." Brenda banged the table, too.

"Sounds sensible," Sam J. muttered.

"You know what I think." Mrs. Binder set the teapot down hard on the stove.

We finished dinner in thoughtful silence, giving her pork the attention it deserved.

At seven thirty, half an hour before my fellow wise people were due to dance lightly through the front door, I stretched out on the living room couch trying to memorize some opening remarks to get my decision across.

"It has come to my attention," I said mentally,

"that my honor and integrity have been questioned..."

No. Only *I* had questioned them so far, I reminded myself.

For a moment I pictured Reed's face when he yanked his helmet off. Of course, it was twisted into a loathsome mask of hate and vengeance. But just before it got that way, Reed looked a little like Bob does sometimes when Brenda pulls a trick he never expected. Right before Bob starts crying his expression seems to say, "Is it really possible."

It did not take long to get *that* image out of my mind and try another beginning for my opening remarks.

"It's come to my attention that certain rumors..."

No.

"The *last* thing I want is for anyone to make fun of this court for being influenced by personal emotions. I *especially* don't want this to happen because of me. That's why I'm not giving any opinion at all..."

Good.

"Can I talk to you a minute?"

I opened my eyes at the sound of Maddie's voice. She sat beside me on the couch. Wonderful. Another heart-to-heart chat. How many more could I take?

Still, I was sort of glad to see her. I assumed Mrs. Binder had complained about my wearing an old dress to the wedding, and made Maddie promise that she'd drag me around town to get a new one. I concentrated on being gracious.

That's a lovely idea, Maddie, I silently improvised. *I'd be delighted to join you whenever you have a free moment.*

"Listen," she said, "you're making a mistake."

I said nothing, mentally or otherwise.

She went on. "I know you're trying to handle this situation in a strict, honest way, but you are selling yourself short."

Her moist gold-brown eyes glittered with the light of the end table lamp. Beneath her spare makeup I could see the lines of a hard day's work at the corners of her eyes and her mouth.

"Let me tell you a story," she said.

Maddie shifted to get more comfortable. I moved, to help her. She said, "Some years ago, when I began in the Personnel Department of Shore Foods, I had to consider applicants for a junior executive position. Several of them seemed very qualified. I had a ... reaction to one of them. I liked him very much. In fact, I hoped I'd see more of him at the company if he came to work for us."

Maddie's eyes glittered a little more brightly as she remembered. I realized my mouth was open so I closed it.

"I was also quite sure in my own mind that this young man was outstanding material for the job. But my boss was even more impressed with another candidate and told me he planned to recommend his choice. Then he asked if I wanted to review his decision with him.

"I knew my boss would listen fairly. But I also knew he'd ask sharp, probing questions. I pictured myself revealing the fact that I had a crush on the young man I wanted to recommend. I became convinced that my professional judgment would begin to look ...unreliable."

Maddie paused, mentally reliving the emotions of long ago. I gave her a few seconds for that before curiosity overwhelmed good manners.

"So what happened?" I asked.

"I did not ask to review the decision, or make any objection. My boss's candidate was hired and then let go in a few months."

"Fired? Why?"

Maddie smiled sadly. "He wasn't right for the job. I believe he went into exterminating here in Baltimore."

"What happened to your guy?" I asked.

"He found work in California. Soon, we started reading about him in trade publications reporting his quality control computer studies. Today's he's the President of Golden Gate Foods.

"Not long after I interviewed him, my boss showed me one of the articles I mentioned. It called my candidate a rising star. My boss recognized the name and asked, 'When you interviewed this guy, didn't you spot his talent?'

"I had to admit that I had. And I also had to admit that I was afraid to argue for him because I thought my reasons might not seem objective and professional. It was one of the most embarrassing moments of my life."

"What did your boss say?" I asked.

Maddie took a deep breath and let it out very slowly.

"He told me that if I didn't have as much confidence in my own judgment and in myself as he had, I did not belong in the job."

She paused again, glanced away, and then turned to me with an extremely determined look on her face.

"That teacher of yours may or may not have been justified in tricking you onto this court of his, but I know why he did it."

"Yeah?" I whispered.

"Oh, yes. Apparently he knows you almost as well as I do. He knows that no matter what happens when the judges meet, there will be one person in the room who is willing to search her mind and her soul until she is absolutely convinced that she has done her best to be fair and reasonable, and to follow the rules, and to help everyone else do the same."

She dabbed at her eye with the back of one wrist and said, "There just aren't many people you can rely on for that sort of thing. I don't know exactly what's going on in your very exciting personal life, but I do know this. It won't matter as far as your decision is concerned. So I'm telling you what my boss told me. Kindly have as much faith in yourself as Mr. Bain does, and as I do. And kindly give your fellow judges the benefit of your two cents' worth."

A few seconds later we were hanging on to each other for dear life and I heard Mrs. Binder saying "Shhhussshhh" from the kitchen as Bob whispered, "But they're *crying*."

9.

When Maddie and Sam J. left for the movies, I kissed her goodnight, she kissed me, and Mrs. Binder bellowed "Stardust" from the kitchen to give the impression that she was not snooping.

The kids were already upstairs playing Galloping Gaucho. I suggested Mrs. B. do the same. She continued to tidy the kitchen without looking at me.

"Will you?" I asked.

"Who will serve the cookies?" she wanted to know.

"I will."

She squinted at me. "Are you trying to get me out of the way?"

"Yes," I said.

"I'm shocked." She spread a hand over her heart.

"Well, I'm sorry," I explained. "But it's not such a good idea for you to stick your opinions in. You have a very forceful personality and you might influence the judges' opinions, and we're not supposed to be influenced by anything except what we heard in the courtroom. Not even by the wisdom of older and smarter people like you." I followed her into the living room, where she pretended to dust.

Mrs. B. tried to ignore the issue. "What about a dress for the wedding?"

"We're going to buy one next Wednesday," I said, nodding toward the stairs, which I wanted her to climb.

"I'll keep my thoughts to myself," she promised.

I nodded more vigorously at the stairs.

She shook her head. "If I feel the need to set any hooligans straight...I'll go upstairs instead. Word of honor."

I thought about that. "Okay."

The front bell rang. Mild shakes began when I opened it and saw Jan. But the look on her face eased my nerves. While she didn't appear quite friendly, she didn't seem hostile, either. I felt sure she had no interest in continuing our fight that evening. She took her seat at the dining room table and opened the notebook in which she'd taken occasional notes during the trial. I hoped she'd at least done her report on specific rule-breaking, despite her contempt for the court. I sat across the table from her but we didn't look into each other's eyes. Skinny Pete Sweeney showed up two minutes later, and Mary Jo Fogel a minute after him.

"I've been giving this case a lot of thought," Mary Jo said importantly.

Pete snorted and then stroked some stringy blond hair from his eyes. "Where's the human handkerchief?" he said. "I don't have all night for this."

Mrs. Binder put a huge plate of Danish butter cookies in the middle of the table and asked charmingly what everyone wanted to drink. I knew she disapproved of Pete Sweeney's gruff request for "black coffee, extra strong," but she smiled supersweetly to show how cooperative she could be.

Just as we decided to start minus Amy Plutzer, the poor thing arrived with a fistful of Kleenex, her nose the color of grape juice.

"I'm not sick," she explained, noticing my dismay when I opened the door. "The virus is better now. It's just an allergy."

"What are you allergic to?" I asked.

She waved her Kleenex around like a bus was leaving. "That's the tragedy. Nobody knows."

She seemed very brave.

We started the meeting with Jan's report on the issue of specific rule-breaking.

"I have to report that the defense did make sort of an okay case," she said. "It looks like some people did break some rules, but I don't care because the rules are stupid."

Next I asked Amy Plutzer to give her report on principles of law. She said, "It's no big deal."

I had to question her further.

She replied, "You heard what Mr. Bain said."

"Yes," I agreed, "but you're supposed to give a

report on which side made a better case on this issue."

Amy blinked her blood-shot eyes. "It was even."

The others started to look impatient.

"How come?" I asked.

Amy blew her nose violently. "The administration didn't have to give the people all that many rights. But it would have been nice if they did. So, if we vote on what they had to do, Ted wins. If we vote on what would be nicer, Reed wins."

I said, "Thank you, Amy."

She blew her nose again.

Pete Sweeney came next with his report on mitigating circumstances.

"I never saw so many mitigating circumstances in my entire life," he yelled. "I don't even think the students should be on trial here, because they're two-hundred-percent innocent."

"They're not on trial," I said. "The administration's decision is being appealed."

"You better believe it!" Pete shouted, twisty teeth showing, eyes flickering with enthusiasm. "What's Bronto supposed to do, anyway? Play badminton with a bunch of freshman girls? And what about that kid Omar from the Dominican Republic? Is he supposed to take first-year Spanish twice when he knows it better than I talk English?"

"Excuse me," Mrs. Binder exclaimed in his ear as she leaned forward to present the black coffee.

Pete went on a while longer. I didn't stop him

because I considered his lunatic rantings entertaining. After he ran out of steam, Mary Jo Fogel talked about alternative penalties while fanning her satiny cheeks with those lush jet lashes.

"This *seems* very simple," she said, "but it isn't. Reed's team only suggested one alternative penalty, a letter of reprimand. That's okay if we agree that changing the program cards was a Mickey Mouse thing, like cutting a class or two. But if we agree that it's more serious, two-day suspension isn't so bad. The administration could've given four."

Surprise showed on Jan's face and outrage on Pete's, but neither spoke.

I had the job of reporting on the overall fairness issue because we'd decided it was the hardest one to talk about and, after all, I was Chief Justice.

First I reviewed the facts of the case. Then I said, "It depends on how you look at it. It's unfair for kids to have to stand around for hours to get their programs changed. But it's also unfair to expect the administration to let people break rules and not do anything about it. But remember, we're supposed to decide whether the administration made a *serious* mistake. That means we can't overturn them unless they were extremely unfair."

"So?" Jan said, ice in her voice.

"So I'm not saying I like what happened. And I'm not saying Benoit is a big sweetheart. But I don't think they were extremely unfair. They did not break their own regulations and they did not give the worst penalties they could have. I don't think we can say they made a serious mistake and failed to do their job."

Almost out of sight in the living room easy chair, Mrs. Binder lowered her newspaper just long enough to shoot me an approving wink. Of course I ignored her. Mary Jo closed her eyes again. Amy wiped her nose. Pete looked at his coffee like there were things floating in it.

"I don't believe this," Jan whispered.

"Well," I sighed, "I don't think it matters what I say. You probably have the majority on your side anyway."

"Right," Jan declared. "All who agree the administration made a bad mistake, raise your hands."

Hers and Pete's were up before she finished. But nobody else's followed.

"Against," I said, raising mine.

Mary Jo couldn't decide. Her arm jerked up and down three or four times before she let it rest at eye level beside her face.

"Is that up or down?" Jan moaned.

"I'm not sure."

"Well, *be* sure," Pete ordered, his nasty tone sending a jolt right through me. Mary Jo straightened in her chair and threw her wide shoulders back. I imagined her as Joan Crawford or some other bygone movie actress playing a millionairess who hates all living things. For several seconds she stared at Pete. When he could no longer stand it and looked to Jan for help, Mary Jo thrust her arm overhead, fingers wiggling for the ceiling. She tossed her head so her rich brown hair resembled a shampoo commercial.

"Well this is hunky-dory," Jan groaned. Then, after punishing Pete with a mean stare of her own, she turned to Amy Plutzer, who had not yet made a move.

Amy sniffled. Pete put down the blue coffee cup, postponing his first sip, and said, "Just a minute, Amy. Before you decide, you should think about two things. First, I know you won't be impressed by the fact that two skeevy chicks at this table are nothing but administration flunkies. Second, I have another argument that nobody's even *thought* of yet."

"It had better be good." Jan warned him.

"It's a really serious overall fairness argument." Sweeney smirked. "The only way the administration ever found out about these program changes was when the school computer *accidentally* discovered them. The phony changes did not, repeat not, not, not, cause any problems. They did not overload any classes with too many kids. They did not keep anyone from getting credits they needed. In fact, the phony changes did a good job of *helping* the administration run the school better."

Delight showed all over Jan's face.

"That's true," I said, "but Reed's team never mentioned it in court. We can't base our opinion just on what we *think*. We can only base it on what we heard in court. If it wasn't in the evidence, we can't really consider it."

"Hah," Pete laughed. "That's a *big* joke coming from *you*."

So there it was at last, squatting like an ugly reptile next to the butter cookies—the subject no one had chosen to mention aloud until that moment.

I caught my breath and said, "What do you mean?"

"You know." He said it as though the whole world knew.

"Tell me," I whispered.

"Simple. You're fooling around with Ted Steele, and that's the *only* reason you're turning against your fellow students. We all know that."

Machine gun fire broke loose in the living room. I turned to see Mrs. Binder bunching her newspaper into a ball with quick, hard slaps. When I turned back to the table, Jan had reached to her right and grabbed the front of Pete's yellow "Surfer's Turf" T-shirt.

Pete Sweeney is not overwhelmingly physical, which is why people call him "The Bone." Also, Jan is very strong, especially for a girl. But I believe it was mainly animal rage that allowed her to jerk Pete Sweeney around like a floppy puppet.

When he squirmed loose, she barked, "Take it back!"

Pete rubbed his chest and stared at the cookies,

breathless and humiliated. Jan gritted through clenched teeth, "Apologize to my friend."

Pete opened his mouth but nothing came out.

"Forget it," I said quickly. "I don't blame you, Pete. It's my fault everyone thinks that."

"I don't think that," Jan said, looking at me as though I were one of my own accusers. She continued, "I don't know where you get your bizarre ideas, but I know it isn't from Ted!" She moved her eyes around the table. "Sandrine may have her head screwed on funny, but she wants to do the right thing and she's nobody's flunky. Not Ted's, not Benoit's. Am I right?"

A faint-looking Amy Plutzer nodded and Mary Jo's eyes blazed. Summoning what seemed like great courage Pete looked at Jan and said, "Does this mean you're changing your mind?"

"No," she replied in a slightly softer tone, "it just means we're supposed to work together, and you owe Sandrine an apology."

Pete stuck out his lower lip to show he was reconsidering. "Well, in that case," he shrugged, "I admit I was a little off-base. In fact...I apologize."

He raised his cup in a toast to me, swallowing for a very long time to show sincerity.

"Thanks," I said, relieved. "Maybe we should vote again."

We did. Amy remained undecided. We worked on her for half an hour. Her nose became leakier as time passed, but she tried her best to concentrate.

Mrs. B.'s coffee turned Pete's face green so he didn't say much after a while.

"I *hate* to make decisions," Amy finally whined in desperation.

"Then why'd you volunteer for judge?" Mary Jo inquired.

"It was a bad decision," Amy confessed. "Can't I just flip a coin?"

I was almost ready to back that suggestion when Mary Jo sang out, "I've got a better idea. How about this?" She shook with pleasure. "We can write *two* opinions. In the first one, we say the administration did not break its own rules or give the kids a worse punishment than it had to, so strictly speaking we cannot say the administration's decision must be overturned.

"But we also write a second opinion. This one says we believe the administration *was* unfair. They forced students to break rules and then *punished* them for doing it. And even though the administration did not break its own regulations, they did a putrid job of handling program changes and we consider *that* a serious mistake, and we think the administration ruling *should* be overturned in favor of sending the students letters, like Reed said."

"That doesn't make any sense," Pete grimaced, greener than ever. "The two opinions disagree."

Mary Jo looked extremely superior. "Don't you see *any* movies besides Brutal Monkeys concerts? Didn't you ever hear of *The Farrago Case*?"

None of us had.

"Well, it's a wonderful picture from the forties," she explained. "Many critics agree Rita Hayworth does some of her best early work in it."

"Get to the point," Jan suggested.

Mary Jo said, "In *The Farrago Case*, the members of the Supreme Court disagree, so they write two opinions. The majority write one opinion, which decides the case. But the other three justices, including Rita's ex-father-in-law, write a minority opinion explaining why they disagree with the majority. And of course, the two lawyers played by Rita Hayworth and Walter Pidgeon merge their law firms and get married."

Everyone looked at me.

"Mr. Bain didn't say we *couldn't*," I told them.

Pete asked Mary Jo, "Which one is the majority opinion and which one is the minority opinion?"

We all looked at Amy Plutzer. I could be wrong, but it seemed to me that Amy flicked her strained eyes toward the living room before dragging those tattered tissues across her nose, pointing a finger at me, and whimpering, "I vote with Sandrine. Can I please be excused?"

She was.

The four of us pitched in writing both opinions. That took another hour. We agreed that Mary Jo would read the majority opinion signed by me, Mary Jo and Amy. Jan said Pete could read the minority opinion.

"Sorry I was so stupid," Pete whispered on the way out.

"Forget it," I said.

"Very interesting," Mrs. Binder observed as I closed the door.

"Listen," I replied. "You didn't give Amy Plutzer any help making up her mind, did you?"

"Amy who?" Mrs. Binder extended her arm for me to pull her out of the easy chair. "You go to bed," she instructed. "I'll keep the door open for your dad."

Jan called the moment she got home.

"Thanks," I said.

"For what?"

I sniffed, wondering if I'd caught something from Amy. "For coming to my rescue when Pete mentioned me and Ted."

Jan replied, "Can you *imagine* the bottom-dweller saying a thing like that?"

"I don't care about him," I said. "I was worried about you after the way we yelled at each other. We never fought that way before."

She made a clicking sound with her tongue. "I know."

"What do you think?" I asked.

Jan didn't answer immediately. After more clicks and breathing noises, she said, "People change. *You're* changing pretty fast. And now you're in a situation where you have to say what you think ... because you think you have to. You can't keep it all to yourself anymore. And I think what *you* think is stupid. So? The closer people are, the more disappointed they get with each other. I've been disappointed with my brothers nonstop since I was five. Aren't you disappointed with me?"

"A little," I said.

"So?"

"That's all?" I pressed.

"I think so," she replied. "It's like you're dressing weird and I'm not so thrilled about it. But what's the difference anyway?"

I wasn't convinced that was *all* there was to it, but I felt reassured enough to change the subject. "Pete isn't the only one," I said. "Lots of people are going to agree with him about me and Ted, especially after they see which opinion I signed."

"That's true," Jan admitted. "But you didn't have any choice, did you? You had to follow your conscience. Even if it's the most twisted one in Maryland, you had to follow it."

"I guess," I agreed.

Jan tried to sound cheerful. "Look at it this way. You stuck up for your clam-dip principles and Ted's gonna be a charm on your bracelet forever and ever: Amen."

"I guess."

"So relax. Who cares what people think?" Jan didn't sound all that convinced herself.

"See you tomorrow," I said.

□ □ □

Even in the dark, I could make out the ceiling clearly. Awaiting sleep, I would gladly have traded my overgrown conscience for a small bottle of cheap nail polish.

Not only was it going to cost me my membership in civilized society, what with everyone in the school about to consider me, Mary Jo and poor Amy Plutzer the three top traitors of the ages, but I also said goodbye to even the faint possibility that Reed and I might someday be friends again.

After discovering me about to conduct my little experiment in Ted's manly arms, and after learning how I had voted on the court, Reed would be convinced more firmly than any human being on the face of the earth that I had sold my honor under the influence of brainless passion. I smiled bitterly with the secret knowledge that the one time I actually kissed Ted Steele, I didn't even like it. Talk about cruel ironies!

Just as I was contemplating that one, the angel of irony dropped another dilly on my pillow. I would never kiss Ted again. It was the only way left. Nobody would believe I acted honestly while Ted and I were still a big item at school. Even if Ted begged me to continue our friendship secretly, I vowed to say no. Someone would *have* to find out. Then I'd be so covered with shame and disgrace I wouldn't live it down till past forty.

I decided to tell Ted as soon as I saw him.

No Ted. No Reed. Only me...alone.

Drowsing and drifting, I pictured the field the

way it had been two weeks ago, when Jan and I watched jumping jacks, salty air sharp, sky bright blue.

Reed bent forward guarding the goal, left foot turned slightly outward as always. One of the players rushed from the pack. Reed slid sideways to block the ball. A second attacker shot. Reed dropped his stick to block the ball bouncing in front. Then Ted tore out of the pack like a cyclone, whirling around a defenseman guarding him, one glove holding his stick in the clear, throwing the huge defenseman off balance, clutching the stick in both hands, shooting...

My dreamy focus shifted to Reed. I saw the goal as a six-foot-square trap. He was stuck there with no escape, the same way I was stuck. The goalie could not run away. He could not even duck. He had to jump in front of the ball every time it came at him, no matter how fast or how often. I knew how he wished he could cover the field like a blast of wind, slicing the air with his stick as he ran, breathing hard, thinking of scoring goals. It wasn't in him, though. He had something different to do—something few others would even try. Without the goalie, I caught myself thinking, there wouldn't be any game at all. I wished I could *give* him the game tomorrow afternoon.

A tear sizzled down the side of my face as fear bubbled up from the depths of my mind, and I fell asleep praying not to awaken trapped in the "black hole of woe" again.

10.

I dreamed the Galloping Gaucho stood trial for something or other and I defended him. Rita Hayworth was the judge, except she kept changing from Mrs. Binder into Mary Jo Fogel and back again.

Maddie was the witness. The judge would not let me ask any questions until I revealed the Galloping Gaucho's true identity.

"Can't," I explained. "Haven't met him yet."

"Well, get up and get going," the judge said over and over. Of course, it was really Mrs. Binder's voice waking me up.

"Didn't your alarm go off?" she wanted to know.

I yawned. "Must've slept through it."

"Well, hurry now. You're late. And don't go back to sleep or I'll pour water in your ear."

"Thank you, ma'am."

Halfway to the bathroom, I realized that far from staggering around in a "black hole of woe," I felt a mixture of excitement, curiosity and fear. It felt a lot like before I went water-skiing for the first time, when I was twelve.

At first I decided to put on my most shapeless gray sweater, so as not to attract any more attention than I could help—considering that I faced social ostracism and the final collapse of my personal life. Then I spied a bright red turtleneck jersey at the bottom of the drawer. I'd never quite had the nerve to wear it before. I stared at it until Mrs. B. yelled that my Wheatina was ready and I wasn't too grown up for an earful.

"Listen," I said to myself. "Let's go down in flames."

I met Jan at the corner in front of Lou's Greekburger Heaven.

"You could change your vote," she said as we neared the school. "The world will still get to hear what you really think, but you won't get the grief for it."

"Only Mary Jo and Amy Plutzer will," I replied.

"True," sighed Jan. "But neither of them has your particular problems."

"Such as?"

"Well, Mary Jo is only interested in her acting career and besides, the way she looks it wouldn't matter if she signed something in favor of cramps. And all Amy Plutzer cares about is her health. But you..."

"What *about* me?"

She worked up a weak smile. "Well, you do have Reed to consider."

"How absurd," I mocked. "Ha-ha." I wasn't trying to fool anyone. I was trying to hold my spirits together.

My first unpleasant order of business was telling Ted the painful truth. Usually, I'd see him half a dozen times in the halls, but today I only caught two fleeting glimpses of Ted and he was rushing both times.

Ironically, I had the feeling that Reed was keeping an eye out for me. Naturally, I stayed away. The *last* thing I needed was his making me an emotional zombie with a day full of accusations. "Cheap, rotten, corrupt," I said to myself as I ducked around corners and sped down stairs to avoid him.

And I succeeded.

By the time I sat behind the judges' table to face the worst in my turtleneck, I had said not a single word to Reed *or* Ted. I had, however, gotten in a brief conversation with Mr. Bain just outside the Small Auditorium. At first, he did not look very thrilled when I told him we had two opinions instead of one.

"The Supreme Court does it," I explained. "Didn't you ever see *The Farrago Case?*"

That jiggled his eyebrows, all right.

"Yes," he said. "Have you?"

"What's the difference?" I answered rather snappily. "If it's good enough for Rita Hayworth and Waldo Pidgeon, it's good enough for me."

"Oh, is it really?" He bent his head forward to check me out over his glasses.

"Listen," I said, "if you let us do it our way, I'll forget that you tricked me into being Chief Justice, and we'll be even."

"Difficult offer to turn down," he nodded.

I headed for my chair and, a few minutes later, Mr. Bain explained to the large crowd that the panel had split and would read a majority *and* minority opinion.

Mary Jo announced that she, Amy and I had signed the following. Then she read our half-page opinion which told why we could not recommend that the administration's decision should be overturned and the suspensions revoked.

Following Ted Steele's lead, his victorious team of Arnold Playfield and Lisa Hooper stood in the front row to receive the applause of the crowd. Needless to say, there wasn't any. Instead, all three caught some pretty crude remarks about their appearances and personalities, especially for a courtroom.

Considering which side I was on, it wasn't easy to pound my gavel for order in the court. But I did, and miraculously, nobody flung any foul language up at me.

Then Pete Sweeney stood. His slightly-too-small blue blazer and Day-Glo red tie inspired scattered whistles. He feasted on the attention until Jan jerked his jacket.

Once Pete started reading, I realized we should have pretested him for ability. Unfortunately, Pete pronounced about a dozen words wrong and stopped in the middle of practically every sentence. With Jan whispering up to correct him, however, the audience got the point.

And, naturally, they loved it. When he finished, Pete waved to the cheering crowd. Reed hauled his defeated colleagues Richie Green and Sheila Dufay to their feet to share in the glory. I let everyone cheer as much as they wanted, which was a lot. Even those few kids who agreed with our majority opinion loved hearing Dean Benoit being pummeled in public. So did I.

After that, Mr. Bain stood and thanked everyone again, especially the five judges. Then, Dean Benoit came up to say that we had honored the memories of Maxwell and Francine Small, a wealthy but deceased local couple who paid for the Small Auditorium in exchange for putting their bronze replicas on a plaque outside the door. Then the Dean asked us to give Mr. Bain a hand for being such a brilliant and devoted teacher. It was a little on the feeble side, I thought, but he seemed to enjoy it.

Mr. Bain ended the session by reminding the members of our Law and Democracy class that they'd have to hand in their two-page opinions on Monday. He asked me to bang the gavel once more to make everything official, and I did.

Instead of leaving, lots of kids crowded around Reed, his lawyer team, Jan and Pete Sweeney. I didn't expect congratulations for winning, so I wasn't disappointed. All I wanted to do was find Ted, break the news, and then wander off to begin my new life as a female hermit.

Mercifully, the kids in the audience pretty much ignored me in their eagerness to congratulate all the new heroes.

Amy, Arnold and Lisa Hooper stood around waiting for a kind word from somewhere. Mary Jo got lots of attention from several paralegal students who had eyeballed her all week.

Where was Ted?

I found him just outside the Small Auditorium, accepting the adulation of that enthusiastic redhead I have already mentioned. Although I did not expect him to go to blubbering pieces, it did feel a little awkward rejecting Ted in front of a third party. Still, I wanted desperately to get it over with.

Of course, it already was over, as I should have known.

"Ted," I said. "Can I speak to you privately?"

The redhead seemed to mistake me for a talking flatworm.

"Hey," Ted smiled. "Great job on the court. Really neat opinion. I appreciate the effort."

That was it.

I thought for a moment about calling him some of the names I quickly imagined Jan suggesting. No, I told myself, with a monopoly on cheap, rotten and corrupt, why add tacky, gutter-mouthed and sore loser?

I made the first turn I came to with tears stinging

the corners of my eyes. It wasn't that I minded losing Ted. I'd already made up my mind that I did not want him. It wasn't that I felt humiliated. I did not care what the redhead thought.

But Ted's indifference hurt me just the same. I meant absolutely nothing to him at all. But that was only part of it. I realized then, as I had not before, that something was missing from Ted. Throughout his life, people would like him and trust him, and help him and love him too. But he would not understand. So he would disappoint them all, and worse. It hurt me just knowing that. I wondered how many Teds there were in the world, how many I'd meet, and how I'd know who they were.

I'd never felt more alone in my life. And I'd never hated loneliness more. Yet all I wanted was someplace to go where nobody would find me.

I knew the playing field would still be empty for a while. The idea of the open, green expanse attracted me. I wanted to feel alone physically, just as I did emotionally.

Passing through the basement hall where Reed and Ted had battled for what I had innocently assumed to be the prize of my affections, I decided to quit Vocabulary Club.

Walking out onto the field, I considered transferring to McHenry High and beginning a new existence altogether, but decided that would be carrying cowardice too far.

"Hey."

At the sound of his voice, I felt like a gang of

escapees from the crabcake factory were sharpening their claws against the inside of my stomach.

I turned to see Reed Hobart trotting toward me as fast as his bad foot would permit.

Just as well, I told myself. Why shouldn't this day end with him demolishing my self-respect once and for all?

But oddly enough, the fact that I had on my red turtleneck made me feel slightly brave, as though I might actually survive this final onslaught without sinking into the worst depression since 1932.

Reed didn't look angry. He didn't look amused, either. In fact, I'd never seen him look anything like the way he did then. Agitated. And something else which gave me a strange melting feeling. It started in my throat and wasted no time spreading through me.

"This is it," he announced out of breath. "I'm going to tell you exactly how I feel and you can laugh all the way home if you want, but at least I won't have to live any more like a gutless wimp jellyfish without the courage to say it."

His breathing leveled off, but the fire in his eyes did not. "Just don't say another word," he said.

Not that I planned to.

He went on, looking down at me from not too many inches away.

"I've been unbalanced about you since August. I swear I have thought about you every day and every night since Ron introduced us.

"I kept telling myself you were Ron's girl and he was my friend, but I knew that wasn't the reason I held back. I was scared to find out you didn't feel the same way. I guess I should've waited till you got him out of your system, but I was hating myself too much, calling myself a coward and all. So I promised myself I'd do something on my birthday, which is November seventh when I asked you to go to the movies and you turned me down. I know it's not your fault and I don't hold it against you, but I got depressed for a whole month after that and I didn't have the guts to ask anymore 'cause I knew it would just happen again. You want to hear something *really* funny? I only joined Vocabulary Club 'cause you were in it."

The tingling warmth I felt then was no blush.

"When Ted started hitting on you it made me nuts. Not only because I hated to think of you with somebody else, but also because I know the kind of guy he is and why he was after you. I mean he's not sincere. If he hurt you I'll go mangle him right now, or at least I'll try. But how could I say anything? If I did I'd look just like Ted, like I was out for myself, to win this stupid Court of Appeals.

"If I told you all this while the trial was on you'd probably think I was just like him. It would have been wrong to mix everything up like that. So just tell me, what could I do?"

Not that I could have made a sensible sound.

Reed didn't wait for one. "I admit I went a little

haywire, insulting you in Vocabulary Club and trying to punch Ted out which probably made me look more like a fool than ever. But I was confused and upset. Is that a crime? Tell me *you* never get confused."

"But..." I began, needing to hear him say only one thing more.

Reed read my mind. "Oh, sure," he said. "A lot of people think Ted got to you and twisted your mind so you'd help him out. So? People used to think the world was flat. What can I do?"

Then he added, "Okay. If it makes any difference to you, I never believed it. When you think about someone every day and night, you get to know what they're like. Believe me, I know. Besides, I had more important things to think about, seeing you with him every day, worrying about you, turning myself inside—"

I twitched my finger for Reed to bend down. When he did, I stood on my toes, and let him know how completely he'd won his appeal.